JULIE ANN GODSON

Julie Ann Godson

Scandal in High Society *Oxfordshire*

Twenty tales of toffs in trouble

FeedARead.com

First published in 2017 by FeedARead.com

ISBN 9781786972859

A CIP catalogue record for this title is available from the British Library.

Front cover: "The Love Letter", Pio Ricci (1850–1919)
Back cover: Detail from "The Death of Amy Robsart"
by William Frederick Yeames (1835–1918)
Picture credits: Pages 11, 33, 34, 38, 47, 67, 80, 122 National Portrait Gallery; 12 Penshurst Place; 19 The Ditchley Foundation; 23 Savvy Group; 26, 40, 41, 43, 94, 117 National Trust; 28 Ray Main/SWNS.com; 32 Stephen Dorey; 37 newbury.net; 38 mapio.net; 48 Fowler Architecture and Planning; 63 York Museums Trust; 66 Royal Collection Trust/© Her Majesty Queen Elizabeth II 2016; 66 National Gallery of Victoria, Melbourne; 69 TVCHP; 71 WI; 82 Fitzwilliam Museum; 85, 114 telegraph.co.uk; 87 West Wycombe Park, Buckinghamshire; 100 www.britainexpress.com; 101, 118 National Library of Wales; 102 Kingston Museum and Heritage Service; 106 rightmove.co.uk; 107 Ulster Museum; 122 Chris Wood; 124 British Library; 134 Martyn Ferry; 149 Barney Walters; 158 melbourneblogger.blogspot.co.uk

For Judy

Contents

Introduction

THIS COLLECTION of true stories came about because I was asked to speak on a subject of local historical interest at a dinner in the summer of 2017.

While researching my book *The Water Gypsy: how a Thames fishergirl became a viscountess* I came across many entertaining tales of real-life iniquity, misconduct and plain criminality involving the aristocracy, so I parked them all carefully on my computer for use in some as yet unspecified project. At last, their time has come.

I felt I owed my reader the duty of avoiding tedious bunching of aristocratic transgression; a run of chapters on dispiriting adultery followed by a succession of self-seeking murders might be grim. So I started by arranging the stories chronologically just to see what happened, and to my surprise no bunching was evident. I can only conclude that the sheer variety of ways in which the upper classes of Oxfordshire have contrived to behave badly over the centuries is nothing less than impressive.

Long may their efforts continue.

Julie Ann Godson
2017

1
The suspicious death at Cumnor Place

LAUGHING AND HAPPY, the servants of an ancient manor house tumbled back from Abingdon fair late one summer afternoon in 1560 to find a shocking scene. At the foot of the stairs lay their young mistress, her neck broken. On the back of her head were nasty wounds, possibly blows, the worst being a full two inches deep. Amy Robsart was twenty-eight years old, and seemed to be the girl with everything. But Queen Elizabeth I wanted Amy's husband for herself.

Cumnor Place pictured in the early 1800s: it was demolished shortly afterwards

Amy was born into a life of privilege; at the age of seventeen she married up-and-coming star and Elizabethan Court dream-boat Robert Dudley, and her marriage was a love-match. So why, ten years later, was poor Amy found dead at Cumnor Place, with rumours swirling that she had been murdered on the orders of her beloved husband?

The daughter of Sir John Robsart of Syderstone in Norfolk, Amy was said to be quiet and charming. She grew up at her mother's home Stanfield Hall, also in Norfolk. On 5th June 1550, Amy married Robert Dudley at the palace of Sheen at Richmond at a ceremony attended by Henry VIII's children King Edward VI and Princess Elizabeth.

Robert Dudley was the sixth son of the mighty Duke of Northumberland. Robert and Amy's marriage began happily in Norfolk, but Robert soon acquired a taste for Court life and the opportunities it offered. He even became involved in the failed scheme to put his sister-in-law Lady Jane Grey on the throne. Loyal Amy visited her husband during his year of imprisonment in the Tower of London.

Dudley was a childhood friend of Queen Elizabeth; they had been pupils in the royal schoolroom together. When Elizabeth came to the throne in 1558 she made Dudley Master of the Queen's Horse, a post which apparently necessitated the pair spending long hours giggling alone together in the Queen's rooms, plus his own apartment positioned immediately next door to hers so that the pair might visit one another, apparently "day and night". It was not customary for the wives of courtiers to live at Court, and Amy appears to have endured a somewhat peripatetic existence, moving between the houses of her husband's clients, such as Anthony Forster at Cumnor Place.

In the meantime, the Queen showed no inclination to marry any of the suitors paraded before her. Naturally the gossip began. The Spanish ambassador quoted in a report to his master at home in Madrid the rumour that Dudley intended to divorce his wife or even poison her in order to marry the Queen.

Then, lo and behold, on 8th September 1560 Amy was found dead after a fall down the stairs at Cumnor. Was it an accident, or something more sinister? The rumour-mill at Court went into overdrive. Obviously, the story went, Dudley's inconvenient wife had been done away with so that the Queen could marry her favourite.

So could Amy really have been disposed of so that Dudley was free to marry the Queen? Perhaps one of Dudley's agents bashed Amy on the head and shoved her down the stairs to make her head injuries look accidental? The coroner's report detailed the horrifying dents in Amy's skull, the worst two inches deep.

The Spanish ambassador had reported in the previous April that:

Robert Dudley, afterwards first Earl of Leicester: said to be "splendid in appearance". A well-attributed portrait of Amy Robsart has yet to be found

"[Dudley's] wife has a malady in one of her breasts and the Queen is only waiting for her to die to marry Lord Robert." If Amy had died of natural causes, a respectably-widowed Dudley would have stood a reasonable chance of re-marrying to the Queen. But Dudley knew well that the apparent convenience of Amy's demise would now create an enduring whiff of suspicion around him that would make it quite impossible for him ever to be considered as a royal consort. Would he really take the risk of blowing his chances just to expedite matters by a few months?

It could still have been murder, and for exactly the same reason. There was somebody else who might benefit by the helpful timing of Amy's death. Dudley's foremost rival at Court was William Cecil, Lord Burghley. The Queen's chief advisor resented Dudley's growing influence over the Queen, and marriage would certainly have elevated Dudley's importance above his own. If it was known that Amy was ill, better to hurry things along a bit and make her death look like a crime than allow the girl to die naturally and leave the way open for Dudley to become a figure of sympathy in a position to marry the Queen without suspicion.

Queen Elizabeth I dancing the Volta with Robert Dudley, Earl of Leicester

"The Death of Amy Robsart" as imagined by Victorian artist William Frederick Yeames

To concentrate on choosing between Dudley and Burghley as instigators of Amy's death would be to ignore the gritty realities of the time. Queen Elizabeth was constantly urged by her council to marry in order to acquire an heir. But the hazards of Tudor childbirth meant that marriage by no means guaranteed the royal succession. It was all very well for a king; if his queen died, he could simply re-marry and try again. Not so simple for a ruling queen. Infant mortality was high; a queen might have to endure the unpredictable process repeatedly before producing a healthy child likely to survive to adulthood. She might die in childbirth, leaving an infant monarch and an unstable Protectorate in place. She and the child might die at the same time, leaving chaos behind where the mother had been the monarch and the child her heir. The best way to control the succession from Elizabeth's point of view would be to remain a virgin queen and nominate the most appropriate successor from among the available candidates when the time came.

So if we rule out murder, perhaps Amy had simply had enough of her rather sad existence. We don't know for sure whether the rumours concerning Robert Dudley and the Queen reached Amy at Cumnor, but she was said to be depressed and agitated on the day of her death. Was she so unhappy that she simply decided to end her own life? Amy hadn't seen her husband for a year at the time of her death and she may have been aware that she was heading for what, at the time, would have been an agonising death as a result of the lump in her breast.

Certainly, Amy made sure that she was alone in the house on the day of her death. She insisted that her servants take the day off to attend Abingdon fair, and even became testy with one lady who declined to go. But would throwing oneself down the stairs be the method of choice for suicide?

Tudor ladies would have been well aware of the properties of the various plants and herbs available in the gardens at Cumnor Place and in the countryside around. Although guaranteeing an unpleasant death, taking

poison would still have been quicker than lingering for months with breast cancer.

Those who doubt the suicide theory point to the order placed by Amy a couple of weeks before her death for a splendid new gown. And throughout his year of absence, Dudley continued to send his wife choice gifts from London. Perhaps, after all, Amy simply tripped awkwardly on the stairs in her long skirts, cracking her head a couple of times on the stone balusters on the way to the bottom.

Amy Robsart's body was taken in a procession to Worcester College in Oxford, followed by eighty poor men and women as well as a choir, assorted members of the University, and heralds. Her funeral cost Rob-

Amy's last letter to her tailor, William Edney

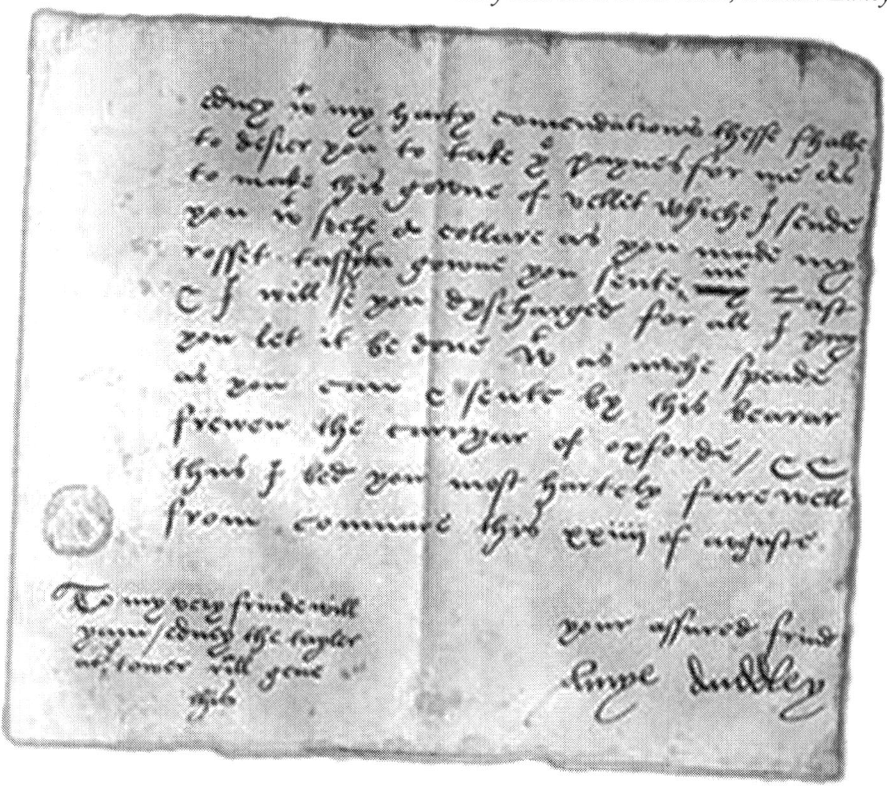

ert five hundred pounds, but he was not present. The chief mourner, by custom of the same sex, was a relative of Forster's wife. After this Amy was buried in the University Church of Saint Mary the Virgin.

Of course, the Queen and Dudley never did marry. In 1564, in anticipation of Elizabeth's plan to marry him to Mary Queen of Scots, she made Dudley Earl of Leicester and granted him Kenilworth Castle as well as extensive property in north Wales. But in 1578 he secretly married Lettice Knollys, widow of the Earl of Essex. When Elizabeth found out about the marriage she was furious, and she treated Lady Leicester with appalling discourtesy for the rest of her life.

By August 1588 Dudley was back in favour, commanding the army at Tilbury when Elizabeth made her famous speech as the Spanish Armada approached English shores. Later that month an exhausted and sickly Dudley set off for Kenilworth on his way to a spa for a cure. But he got no further than Cornbury Park, where he died on 4th September.

The tomb of Robert Dudley, Earl of Leicester, and his second wife Lettice Knollys in the Collegiate Church of St Mary in Warwick

2
The witchfinder of Studley Priory

AN OLD WOMAN named Elizabeth Jackson trembled before judge John Croke of Studley Priory late in 1602. She was accused of bewitching a young girl, and now Croke, as chief legal officer of the City of London, was staging a series of ordeals at his lodgings in the Inner Temple to test the matter. It was not going to be pleasant.

An eminent lawyer and judge, Croke had risen to the posts of Recorder of London and Speaker of the House of Commons in Queen

Studley Priory in about 1640: the site of a Benedictine nunnery between 1184 and 1538

Elizabeth's final Parliament. His grandfather had purchased the Studley estate, originally the site of a convent for Benedictine nuns, in 1539. Fifty years later, Croke built his house around the original priory buildings.

Widow Jackson, on the other hand, was a washerwoman living in the Upper Thames Street area in the City of London. She was, by any standards, a woman of fiery temper—though it may be that, like vulnerable, unprotected women throughout the ages, she had found that some kind of weapon was necessary in a world that loves to target those thought least likely to fight back. For, tellingly, Elizabeth referred to her accuser, a gossip named Mary Glover, as "one of myne enemies", suggesting that Elizabeth was accustomed to being the focus of such idle sport.

Mary was the fourteen-year-old daughter of a well-connected London shopkeeper of the Puritan persuasion. Her uncle was an alderman of the City. Some dispute had arisen between the two women over the clothes of Jackson's daughter, as well as the fact that Mary had subsequently spread tittle-tattle about the matter.

One day, when Mary was despatched on an errand to Elizabeth's house, Elizabeth admitted her and then locked the door behind her. In spite of her lowly social status as a mere charwoman, Elizabeth's seniority in terms of age would, at the time, have entitled her to admonish a young girl, albeit one from a higher social rank than herself. So she proceeded to berate Mary, shouting curses and wishing upon the girl an evil death. A badly-shaken Mary was then allowed to leave.

Three days later, Mary began to suffer from strange and unexplained symptoms. She had difficulty in swallowing, though strangely she did not lose weight. She was struck blind and dumb—though not so dumb that she could not croak "hang her, hang her" whenever Elizabeth Jackson hove into view.

Mary's people were not without means, and several eminent physicians were called in over the following months, but none succeeded in curing the mysterious malady. Mary's seizures and fits in the presence of

Jackson became something of a local attraction, with the Glover household overwhelmed by the curious, the gullible, the awestruck (mainly Puritans), and the sceptical.

The Bishop of London, Richard Bancroft, was among the latter category. As a representative of the established Anglican church, Bancroft was keen to undermine the growing influence of extreme Puritans who were beginning to win support with their hysterical assertions that Satan was abroad in the land in the shape—by and large—of little old

Sir John Croke of Studley Priory

Both the accused, the elderly Elizabeth Jackson, and the accuser, young Mary Glover, were ordered to undergo ordeals before Sir John

ladies. He ordered Croke to establish whether Mary was shamming. At this stage, therefore, both women were under suspicion, and both must undergo testing. They were summoned to the Recorder's lodgings.

First on was Mary Glover. Croke decided to have a third party disguised in Elizabeth Jackson's clothes, and then observe Mary's reaction when the woman approached and touched her. Mary remained impassive. Then the real Elizabeth was wheeled on, and Mary fell into her by now customary writhings.

The next test to establish whether Mary's affliction was genuine involved examining her reaction to deliberately-inflicted pain. If Mary failed to react, it was reasoned, her condition must be supernatural. Croke applied a hot pin to Mary's cheek, and held her hand against burning paper. No reaction. He did it all again. Still no reaction. When the same test was applied to Elizabeth Jackson, she screeched in agony.

So now Elizabeth stood before Croke in a state of terror. Her cries of

Mary could be relied upon to fall into a writhing fit whenever Elizabeth was present

Sir John used hot pins and burning paper to test the nature of Mary Glover's affliction

pain had been construed as proof that Mary was not faking. Elizabeth knew that she was in deep trouble. Unsurprisingly, when Croke barked at her to recite the Lord's Prayer, she fluffed the line "deliver us from evil". When she was obliged by Croke to repeat it, Mary Glover had another of her well-timed fits and once more conquered her dumbness to wheeze in her special spooky voice, "Hang her, hang her."

Croke, at first a sceptic, was now convinced that Elizabeth Jackson had bewitched Mary Glover. Elizabeth's full trial was set to take place on 1st December 1602 at the Old Bailey. She was not without supporters there. But the physicians who testified that Mary's malady was simply a natural illness were unable to convince the court.

The directions of the judge to the jury were less than encouraging for Elizabeth. Sir Edmund Anderson intoned helpfully: "The land is full of witches, they abound in all places. I have hanged five or six-and-twenty of them. There is no man here can speak more of them than myself; few of them would confess it, some of them did against whom the proofs were nothing so manifest as against those that denied it." Elizabeth Jackson was found guilty and sentenced to a year's imprisonment and several sessions in the pillory.

However, this was not the end of the story. Elizabeth was quickly released from prison thanks to powerful supporters. Mary Glover continued to suffer from fits, but two weeks after the trial a group of Puritans cured her with a session of prayer and fasting. To his great discredit, a cowardly Croke sent naïve young Puritan divine Lewis Hughes to deliver the news to Bishop Bancroft. Of course, it confirmed the Bishop's worst fears over handing a moral victory to the Puritans. Hughes endured the full blast of the Bishop's displeasure, and was suspended from his position as curate at St Helen's Bishopsgate.

By contrast, Sir John Croke was knighted in the following year. He became deputy to the Chancellor of the Exchequer in 1604 and, after also serving as a Welsh judge, he was made one of the justices of the Court of King's Bench in 1607. He performed his judicial duties for nearly thirteen years, and died in January 1620.

Studley Priory remained in the Croke family until 1870

3
The outlaw of Cornbury Park

WHAT COULD POSSIBLY be more peaceful, less touched by scandal, than the glorious Botanic Gardens at Oxford? Passing under the Danby Gate, the grand arch at the entrance, to the tranquillity of the blooms and the birdsong within, one might never guess that the founder Henry Danvers, Earl of Danby, was outlawed for murder.

By 1621, when the gardens were founded, Henry Danvers had been at Cornbury Park for four years. The park was granted to Danvers in his capacity as Ranger of the Royal Forest of Wychwood, a grace-and-favour position bestowed on Henry by King James I. In 1626 he was created Earl of Danby by Charles I, and in 1628 he was sworn a member of the Privy Council. It was an astonishing turnaround.

When Henry fled to France as an outlaw in 1594, his future looked bleak. A long-running feud involving the eminent Danvers and Long families had culminated in murder. The origins of the feud are unclear, and may have been rooted in rival Court loyalties—the Danvers to Elizabeth's favourite Essex, and the Longs to Sir Walter Raleigh. But this latest flare-up involved two Danvers brothers, Sir Charles and Henry, against two Long brothers, Sir Walter and Henry.

The father of the Danvers brothers, Sir John, was a magistrate and he had committed one of Sir Walter Long's servants to trial for robbery. Sir Walter sprung his servant from the lock-up, so Sir John Danvers had Sir Walter himself locked up in the Fleet prison. Walter's younger brother Henry Long wrote insulting letters to Sir John's son Sir Charles Danvers calling him "an ape, puppie, foole and boy", and promised that he would whip his bare backside with a rod. This was too much for Sir Charles.

On Friday 4th October 1594, Sir Charles and his brother Henry Danvers, both then in their twenties, went to Corsham where the Longs were lunching with a group of magistrates. Accompanied by some eighteen retainers carrying swords, the Danvers boys crashed in and inter-

Henry Danvers, first Earl of Danby: outlawed for murder at the age of twenty-one

rupted the meal. Sir Charles sought out Henry Long, cudgelled him and then tried to leave. But Henry Long drew his sword and wounded Sir Charles. Hot-headed young Henry Danvers rushed to the defence of his brother Sir Charles. In an instant, Henry shot Long dead.

The Danvers brothers rode like the wind all day and right through

Henry Wriotheseley, Earl of Southampton: patron of William Shakespeare

the following night to Whitley Lodge near Titchfield, property of their friend the Earl of Southampton, arriving at eight or nine in the morning on Saturday 5th. There they laid low for a few days while arrangements were made to get them away. Southampton, who had been celebrating his twenty-first birthday in London, arrived on Monday 7th October. He arranged for the Danvers brothers to journey to Calshot Castle near Cowes from where they sailed for France. There they entered the army of the French King Henri IV.

Sir Charles and Henry Danvers were outlawed, and the incident was said to have hastened the death of their father Sir John. It has also been identified by some as the inspiration for the family feud in Shakespeare's *Romeo and Juliet*. Within two years Danvers supporters were lobbying on Charles and Henry's behalf for their return. Their widowed mother even remarried to a cousin of the Queen, supposedly in the hope of influencing Elizabeth's decision on a pardon for her sons.

In 1597 Henry Danvers was accepted back into the English army to serve during an expedition to Spain. And at the end of June 1598 Queen Elizabeth relented, and pardoned both Danvers brothers on condition that they pay Sir Walter Long fifteen hundred pounds compensation for the murder of his brother. The boys arrived in London eight weeks later.

This was the point at which the fates of the Danvers brothers diverged. In February 1601, throwing in the Queen's face her recent magnanimity towards him, Sir Charles took part in Essex's short-lived rebellion. Charles was convicted of treason and, in spite of offering ten thousand pounds for his life, he was beheaded on Tower Hill on 18th March.

Henry Danvers, the man who seems likely to have fired the shot that killed Henry Long, chose a wiser path. Resisting the lure of Essex and his plans, he served Queen Elizabeth loyally in Ireland. In 1604 he had the sentence of outlawry overturned on a technicality, and in the following year King James I restored him to his disgraced brother Charles's inheritance.

Cornbury Park: originally the grace-and-favour home of the Ranger of the Forest of Wychwood

A succession of lucrative offices and grants followed, including the use of Cornbury Park for life. By Charles I he was created Earl of Danby in February 1626, and he was sworn a member of the Privy Council in 1628. He was installed a Knight of the Garter in November 1633.

His spectacular rehabilitation meant that, on 12th March 1622, Danvers was able to convey to the University of Oxford five acres of land opposite Magdalen College for the purpose of the study of physic and botany. Four thousand loads of "mucke and dunge" were needed to raise the land above the Cherwell flood-plain. The walls were to be as "well fair and sufficient as All Soules College walls, Magdalen Colledge Tower, or any of the fairest buildings in Oxford both for truth and beauty".

According to the *Universal British Directory* of 1791: "The Physic Garden is situated to the south of Magdalen College. We pass through a small court to the grand entrance, designed by Inigo Jones, and executed by Nicholas Stone. It is of the Doric order, and ornamented with rustic

Henry Danvers, Court grandee: he insisted artists always showed the mark on his face

The Danby Gate into the "Physic Garden", now the University of Oxford Botanic Garden

work. It is moreover adorned with a bust of the founder Lord Danby, a statue of Charles I, and another of Charles II. These statues were purchased for 34 pounds."

On the arch is the inscription: "*Gloriae Dei optimi maximi Honori Caroli I. Regis in Usum Academiae et Reipublicae Henricus Comes Danby, Anno 1632*", which translates as, "To the glory of God and the greatest honour of King Charles I Henry Earl of Danby [gave this garden] for the use of both the University and the state in the year 1632."

Henry Danvers, outlaw and murderer, was created first Earl of Danby by Charles I in February 1626. Suffering from poor health in his final years, Henry retired to the country. He died aged seventy at Cornbury Park on 20th January 1644.

4
The unhappy Cavalier of Burford Priory

DURING THE MORNING of 20th September 1643, the first Battle of Newbury had reached a stalemate. Suddenly a young Cavalier galloped out of the front rank of the Royalist line. He raced straight at a gap in a hedge which was lined on both sides by Parliamentarian musketeers. It seemed like sheer madness.

Clever, cultured Lucius Cary, second Viscount Falkland, was born at Burford Priory in around 1609, the son of Sir Henry Cary, first Vis-

Burford Priory: built in the 1580s by Lucius Cary's grandfather, Lawrence Tanfield

count. Lucius's mother was Elizabeth Tanfield, and his maternal grandfather was Sir Lawrence Tanfield, Lord Chief Baron of the Exchequer and owner of Burford Priory.

Lucius's grandfather Tanfield was madly unpopular locally; he was said to have colluded with the local minster to plunder church funds, and to have connived to deprive the burgesses of Burford of their privileges, even using his position to prevent them from finding a lawyer to defend themselves. And tenants on the Tanfields' other estate at Great Tew reported indignantly that Lady Tanfield "saith that we are more worthy to be ground to powder than to have any favour showed to us, and that she will play the very devil among us".

The longevity of the resentment aroused by the behaviour of Lucius's grandparents is suggested by reports that the ghosts of the hated couple may, to this day, occasionally be glimpsed careering around Burford in a flaming coach, bringing certain death upon those who witness the startling spectacle.

Lucius Cary's grandparents were reviled by their tenants in Burford and Great Tew

When Lucius Cary inherited his grandfather's manors in 1625, there was little danger of his following in the Tanfield footsteps as far as his treatment of his tenants were concerned. But relations with his own father Sir Henry Cary were rocky. Sir Henry fiercely opposed Lucius's marriage to Lettice Morison in 1630. But it was a love-match. Lettice was the sister of a friend of Lucius's. Intelligent, pious, and devoted to Lucius, she came to her marriage sadly unburdened by wealth. Perhaps

Lucius Cary, second Viscount Falkland

Lettice Morison: she and Lucius married in secret in the spring of 1630

Sir Henry was disappointed by Lettice's relative impoverishment, but he may also have resented being passed over for the Tanfield estates. So Lucius generously offered to give his inheritance up to his father, but his offer was turned down. This rejection hit the sensitive Lucius hard, and he fled abroad for a while, seeking military service in the rambling and ultimately indecisive Thirty Years War of religion on the Continent.

Educated at both Cambridge and Trinity College Dublin, Lucius Cary was a deep thinker. Having sold Burford Priory in 1634, he made his home at Great Tew and here, in the 1630s, he enjoyed a brief idyll amongst a cultured circle attracted to his house by the proximity of the University and by Lucius's personal charisma. The "Great Tew Circle" of writers and scholars included some of most important intellectuals of the seventeenth century including writer Ben Jonson and historian Edward Hyde, first Earl of Clarendon. Clarendon referred to Lucius as "incomparable", and described a man of "inimitable sweetness and delight in conversation, of so flowing and obliging a humanity and goodness to mankind, and of… simplicity and integrity".

But trouble between King Charles I and Parliament put an end to this tranquil phase of Lucius's life. By now second Viscount Falkland, as well as MP for Newport on the Isle of Wight, Lucius did his best to moderate the King's most unpopular policies whilst remaining loyal to his sovereign. He trod a moderate line in matters of religion, speaking against the interference of the clergy in non-religious business, but at the same time opposing the abolition of bishops.

In January 1642 the faithful Lucius reluctantly accepted the post of King Charles's secretary of state, binding himself yet further into Charles's wrong-headed policies. In June he signed a petition against the King's decision to make war on his own people. And in September he carried Charles's peace overtures to Parliament, emphasising the King's consent to a thorough reform of religion. But the situation was not so simply resolved; Parliament wanted a reform of its own relationship with the monarchy too.

In the following month war broke out, and Lucius Cary fought for the Royalists at the inconclusive Battle of Edgehill. Almost a year later, Lucius was again at the King's side during the unsuccessful siege of Gloucester, fighting with noticeable recklessness.

By this time it was dawning on Lucius that his situation was hopeless. His allegiance to the monarch was an article of faith, but it was also severely shaken by the fatal character flaws of his particular king. At the same time he could not countenance the idea of the divinely-ordained monarch being replaced by Parliament as the supreme power in the land. And the inflexible positions taken up by so many different religious factions caused him nothing but anguish.

Lucius became severely depressed. His friend Clarendon recorded his final relapse into despondency: "His natural cheerfulness and vivacity grew clouded, and a kind of sadness and dejection of spirit stole upon him which he had never been used to…"

On the morning of the first Battle of Newbury in September 1643, Lucius announced forlornly that he was weary of the times, and anticipated much misery in the country. Ominously, he foresaw that he would be out of it all by nightfall. His friends attempted to dissuade him from taking part in the engagement, but to no avail.

Lucius volunteered to serve in the front rank of Sir John Byron's regi-

The moment of Lucius's death: actually he fell with only the enemy around him

ment. Positioned in the centre of the Royalist line, the regiment took Round Hill and forced the Parliamentarians back to a hedge. Lucius spotted a gap in the hedge and galloped straight at it. In the inevitable hail of fire, a shot to the lower abdomen killed Lucius instantly. His body was stripped and left on the battlefield until it was recognised later by a servant, who took it back to Great Tew. Lucius Cary was thirty-three.

Suicide was considered a mortal sin at the time, and it is unclear how successful Lucius was in disguising his wilful self-murder as a valiant act of war. His grave in the village churchyard at Great Tew was significantly unmarked, but at Newbury a handsome monument was erected in his memory.

However, it wasn't Lucius's suicide that was a scandal; it was the fact that such a rational and thoughtful man should be driven to despair by the pig-headed fanatics that surrounded him. A Royalist by instinct, he was nevertheless so frustrated by

Although Lucius's grave at Great Tew is unmarked, this obelisk was erected on the battlefield at Newbury

the intransigence and extremism he found on all sides during the English Civil War that he was driven to take the most desperate of measures.

A heartbroken Lettice devoted her widowhood to treating the sick and dispensing charity to the poor and needy. She built a school at Great Tew where local children were taught literacy and working skills. She died of tuberculosis at Great Tew Manor on 24th February 1647 aged thirty-five.

As a widow, Lettice cast off her finery and donned widow's weeds for the three years that remained to her

Burford Priory today: said to be haunted by two ghosts and a poltergeist

5
The fugitive of Chastleton House

ON A SEPTEMBER night in 1651 the thunder of horses' hooves could be heard in the lane outside Chastleton House near Moreton-in-Marsh. Inside the house, the exhausted Royalist owner Arthur Jones and his anxious wife Sarah made eye contact. They knew that Cromwell's soldiers had only one purpose in mind: to capture Arthur.

Arthur Jones's grandfather Walter acquired Chastleton House in the early 1600s. Walter was an Elizabethan lawyer, though the Jones family's ascent through society derived originally from their trade as successful Welsh wool merchants. The old house at Chastleton was razed to the ground, and the present Jacobean manor was built between 1607 and 1612. It was designed to contain a secret that was about to save Arthur Jones's life.

During the English Civil War between the Crown and Parliament, Arthur Jones elected to fight for the king. By 1651 the Royalists, once sustained by a seemingly endless supply of money, now faced the might of Oliver Cromwell's New Model Army, a disciplined, highly-trained body of men led by officers promoted on merit, and not on account of their blue blood.

On 3rd September 1651 the final battle of the war took place at Worcester. King Charles I had been executed over two years before, and now his son Charles II was supported by the Scots, anxious to restore a Stuart to the throne. Twenty-eight thousand Cromwellian troops comprehensively routed sixteen thousand Royalists. About three thousand men were killed during the battle, although Parliamentary casualties numbered in the low hundreds. A further ten thousand Royalists were taken prisoner at Worcester or soon afterwards.

Royalist Cavaliers who were able to do so scattered and fled, with the Roundheads in hot pursuit. Arthur Jones rode for his life all the

Sarah Jones, née Evans: cool-headed daughter of a London merchant

way from Worcester to Chastleton. He led his exhausted horse into the stables and then, to the relief of his wife Sarah, stumbled out of the dark and into the welcoming warmth of the house.

But the couple's relief was short-lived. Soon came the tramping of boots up to the door. It seemed that Arthur was cornered. Fortunately, for reasons known only to himself, Arthur's grandfather Walter Jones

Arthur Jones: painted from the artist's imagination in the early eighteenth century

Above: the Chastleton estate was bought by the Joneses from Gunpowder Plotter Robert Catesby in the early 1600s

Left: the door to the secret chamber in the tower

had built into the house a secret chamber carefully hidden in the tower over the porch, perfect for just such an eventuality.

While Sarah went to the hall door and tried to persuade the soldiers that her husband was not at home, Arthur bounded up the stairs, opened a hidden door and slipped into the secret room. There he held his breath and strained to hear what was going on below, awaiting his opportunity to flee once more. Downstairs, the Roundheads dismissed Sarah's denials, saying that they had just seen his horse still steaming in the stables. They knew he was at Chastleton somewhere.

However, because it was dark and by now very late, the troops announced that they would wait for morning and perform a proper search in daylight. They chose a room in the tower for their night's stay, and Sarah was commanded to bring food and beer. Unfortunately, the room the soldiers chose housed the only exit from the secret chamber where Arthur was waiting to make his getaway.

The resourceful Sarah went to the kitchens, and used the time out of view of the soldiers to collect her wits. The chatelaine of any country house of the period would have a store of remedies prepared with her own hand from the herbs and flowers in her kitchen garden. Sarah carried a can of ale to her medicine chest and quietly added a good slug of laudanum made from poppies.

Having delivered the ale to her delighted house-guests, Sarah waited

The kitchen where Sarah Jones brewed up something special for her Roundhead guests

outside the door, listening. When the snoring suggested the men had dropped into a drug-induced slumber, she quietly opened the door. Tiptoeing past the comatose Roundheads, she gently pressed the stud which opened the hidden door to the closet where her husband waited.

Arthur emerged quietly, and husband and wife crept back across the room and down the stairs. Arthur immediately made for the stables where, finding the Roundheads' horses fresher than his own, he saddled one up and made his escape.

It seems fair to suggest that anyone quick-witted enough to extricate her husband from such a tricky situation would have no trouble at all in assuming an expression of wounded innocence the following morning when the baffled Roundheads fruitlessly searched the house for the escaped Cavalier.

Arthur Jones was obliged to remain in hiding for a couple of years,

In the morning, the Roundhead soldiers searched the house for the fugitive Royalist

but at the Restoration he planted an oak, which grew into a fine tree once visible from the window of Chastleton's Great Chamber. Arthur lived to a peaceful old age, dying in his late sixties in 1687.

And what of his loyal wife Sarah? She was left an annuity of one hundred pounds a year and the right to live in one half of Chastleton House with her own servants, while her son lived in the other half.

But the fines levied against Arthur by Oliver Cromwell probably set in motion the Jones family's eventual financial downfall. And a decision to back the wrong side once again in the following century hardly helped their financial or political rehabilitation. In the Jacobite rebellion of 1745, the Joneses were staunch Tories, whole-hearted in their support of Bonnie Prince Charlie's attempt to regain the throne for his father James Stuart.

Chastleton House remained in the Jones family for the next three hundred years in a state of increasingly severe disrepair. In 1991 the house passed to the National Trust, and the family left for good.

Chastleton House: now in the hands of the National Trust

6
The king-killer of Longworth Manor

HELL-RAISING, ATHEIST womaniser Harry Marten of Longworth House was not your typical, godly Civil War Parliamentarian. Having reeled drunkenly around Europe on the Grand Tour in the company of his aristocratic friend, the poet Mildmay Fane, Earl of Westmorland, it was said of Harry that he would prefer to command a "regiment of whores" than a "regiment of horse". And, perhaps uniquely, he had a mind to kill both King Charles I *and* Oliver Cromwell.

Harry Marten's birthplace, opposite Merton College chapel

The son of a successful Oxford lawyer and diplomat, Marten was born in his father's house at 3 Merton Street in around 1602. He went up to University College at fifteen years old, graduated at eighteen, and was admitted to the Inner Temple at nineteen. Clearly he was possessed of an above-average brain.

During the Grand Tour that followed his studies, Marten was much impressed by the new philosophical ideas he heard discussed on the Continent. Between bouts of drinking and wenching, he absorbed a new

Harry Marten: republican and regicide

way of thinking that made him a man well ahead of his time, propounding ideas that today we find perfectly reasonable.

At the same time he was described as "a great lover of pretty girles", and his party lifestyle is said to have cost his father a thousand pounds a year. His reputation for wildness earned him the disapproval of King Charles I. Upon spotting Marten at the races in Hyde Park, the King is said to have exclaimed: "Let that ugly Rascall be gonne out of the Parke, that whore-master, or els I will not see the sport." Harry slunk away, but in time he would have his revenge.

In 1627 he married his first wife, with whom he had three daughters. Elizabeth died shortly after the birth of her third child in 1634. A year later he married again. Apparently Margaret Staunton, daughter of a London grocer, was his father's choice, and Harry was somewhat reluctant. However, the couple had three children—two daughters and a son.

In spite of his legal training, during the 1630s Marten was described as merely a 'farmer' of Hinton Waldrist. Alongside his younger brother, George, he managed his father's considerable estate which stretched

Longworth Manor: the estate was acquired by Harry Marten's father for £9,500 in 1618

along the south bank of the Thames and centred on the village of Shrivenham. This was not a great success, and by the outbreak of the Civil War in 1642 the brothers had run up considerable debts.

Marten's reputation as a womaniser probably stemmed from his unconventional decision to live openly with Mary Ward, the sister of the Parliamentarian commander of Tilbury fort. In fact, this was more a manifestation of Marten's contempt for hypocrisy than any deliberate attempt to shock. Harry and Mary may well have been a couple from the time of Marten's first election as a Member of Parliament for Berkshire in 1640, but even this was only after Marten's second wife had born her last child. Harry and Mary certainly considered themselves a couple by 1649, entertaining visiting dignitaries lavishly together and keeping liveried servants. Mary referred to herself, and was referred to by others, as Mary Marten, and this was customary among co-habiting couples. (After Samuel Pepys was widowed, for example, his long-term partner Mary Skinner was generally referred to as "Mistress Pepys".) Harry and Mary had three daughters.

Oliver Cromwell and Charles I: with his customary originality, Harry Marten entertained thoughts of killing both of them

Throughout his parliamentary career Marten enjoyed living high on the hog, but he had some difficulty holding his drink. He turned this to his advantage by feigning drunken slumber in the Commons chamber, then suddenly leaping to his feet to deliver a devastating oratorical blow.

On the outbreak of war in August 1642 he was made governor of Reading. He commandeered sufficient horses to raise a regiment, and commanded a troop in the Berkshire trained bands. During the winter of 1645–6 he acted as commander-in-chief of the infantry at the siege of Donnington Castle.

He was an unshakeable Republican who believed that no country should be ruled by one man, but by a parliament representing the people. One eminent historian describes him as the *enfant terrible* of Parliament. In 1643 he was expelled for expressing the view that it would be better for one family to die—i.e. the royal family—than many. A brief period of imprisonment in the Tower of London inevitably followed.

Although no great friend of Cromwell because of the latter's tendency to resort to the military ahead of an elected parliament, Marten it was who helped him out by coming up with the formula for trying King Charles I. At a meeting of the Commission for the King's trial, Cromwell asked members for suggestions as to how they should deal with Charles's predicted refusal to acknowledge the court's authority to try him. As questions go it was a stinker, and there followed much embarrassed shuffling of papers. At last an exasperated Marten broke the silence: "Why then let it be this: in the name of the Commons and Parliament assembled, and all the good people of England." Greatly relieved, all concurred. After the trial, Marten signed the death warrant of Charles I along with thirty-one other regicides, enjoying a jolly ink fight with Cromwell during the ceremony.

For the first two years of the Commonwealth, Marten was in the thick of state affairs, enjoying a life of wealth and ease. During 1652 he bought Derby House, centre of the state committees, as his private

London house. An award of one thousand pounds a year recognised his expenditure at the state's service. As well as property in Eynsham, he received major parcels of land in Herefordshire and Derbyshire.

When, upon the restoration of Charles II, Marten was put on trial

King Charles showed himself at his best during the worst crisis of his life, losing his stutter during his trial and behaving with great dignity and courage on the scaffold

for his life, he did not deny his principles—nor that he had voted to cut off the King's head. Like his enemy Charles I, he showed a cool-headed courage under the most extreme pressure. Marten was found guilty, but spared execution. This was probably partly because influential Royalists were reluctant to make a martyr out of someone of his personal notoriety, bravery and integrity, and also because he had argued for the lives of Royalists when the Commonwealth wanted retribution.

Marten was imprisoned in the north in 1662, eventually being moved in 1668 to Chepstow Castle. There he remained under a sort of relaxed house arrest for twelve years, with occasional opportunities to travel outside the castle. Mary Ward shared his imprisonment, while his wife Margaret remained in the family home at Longworth with her unmarried daughter Anne to look after her.

On 9th September 1680 Marten died somewhat ingloriously at Chepstow by choking on his supper. No doubt he would point out that it may have been undignified, but it was preferable to choking at the end of a hangman's rope. His quarters were thenceforth re-named after him.

Marten's Tower: built by Roger Bigod, Earl of Norfolk, between 1288 and 1293

7
The highwayman of Chipping Norton

ONE DAY IN 1649, shortly after the execution of King Charles I, a grand coach rumbled down the Great North Road towards London. No less than seven heavily-armed outriders signalled the importance of the personage within. He was the most powerful man in the land, Lieutenant General Oliver Cromwell. At a deserted spot on the route there came the dreaded cry: "Stand and deliver!"

The true Portraicture of Captain *James Hind.*

An early target for Hind: Oliver Cromwell

Considering the odds against them, the two highwaymen must be credited with considerable courage. Cromwell's armed escort immediately set upon them and one, Thomas Allen, was captured and soon hanged at Tyburn. The other, Captain James Hind, rode like the devil and escaped, killing his horse in the process.

In the aftermath of the English Civil War there were many angry Royalist officers, dispossessed of their family lands, roaming a country awash with weapons. Highway robbery offered easy pickings for former soldiers accustomed to handling firearms. The grudge they harboured against the regicides provided a kind of virtuous cloak for what was actually daylight robbery. And their self-image as Cavaliers prompted a good deal of exaggerated gallantry towards the ladies as well as supposed generosity towards the poor. It was all part of the show, and served to win sympathy from a public tired of the joyless rule of the Puritans.

Hind was a Chipping Norton lad. He was a Royalist, but he never had any lands of which to be dispossessed. In fact, his father was a god-fearing saddler of honest reputation who, recognising that his only son was of above-average intelligence, scrimped and saved to send John to grammar school until he was fifteen and old enough to take up an apprenticeship with a local butcher.

James Hind could simply have followed his father into the family saddlery, a business which must have been booming in an age of equestrian warfare. But perhaps he was already too unmanageable for his parents, or perhaps James's Royalist sympathies created a political division within the household between him and his godly father—not an unusual situation at the time.

Claiming that he was badly treated by his butcher master, James begged three pounds of his soft-hearted mother and set off for London. There he applied his efforts to his twin passions of drink and women with admirable earnestness. One night he was carousing in the company of a lady who had relieved a gentleman's pocket of five guineas the night before. She was picked up by the constable and despatched to the lock-up, and Hind was sent with her for good measure.

There he fell into the company of Thomas Allen, a notorious highwayman whose exploits were well known. Celebrating their release the following day, Hind and Allen became firm friends and Allen offered Hind a chance to become his partner in crime. But first he wished to assess young Hind's suitability for the job.

The location chosen for the test was Shooter's Hill to the east of Blackheath—a much lonelier spot then than it is now. Soon a victim appeared: a gentleman accompanied by his servant. Allen hung back to observe how Hind would deal with the situation. Clever Hind knew exactly what was expected of him. Approaching the coach cheerfully, he politely offered at gunpoint to relieve the terrified occupant of all his money. This produced a handsome haul of fifteen pounds. Conscious of his Cavalier obligations, Hind returned his victim twenty shillings that he might complete his journey. Overcome with relief and gratitude (according to Hind) the gentleman swore he would never harm a hair on Hind's head if the highwayman were ever in his power.

Allen was greatly pleased with the bravery and gallant conduct of his new comrade, and the two men swore to stand by one another to the death. Unfortunately for Allen, Hind was obliged to keep his oath of loyalty only until the raid on Cromwell's train. But Hind had learned

Hind impressed his colleague Thomas Allen with his courtesy towards his first victim

enough to maintain a solo career, racking up well-known regicide names among his victims, and furnishing pamphleteers with a plentiful supply of colourful and probably apocryphal stories. His connection with "high society" was that he set out to rob its new crop of grandees.

One alleged victim was Army preacher and regicide Hugh Peter whom Hind encountered in Enfield Chase. No shrinking violet, Peter retaliated against the highwayman's predictable demands by launching a scriptural debate with him. Perfectly well equipped by his fine education to bandy biblical quotes with anyone, Hind responded: "Pray, sir,

Army preacher Hugh Peter

make no reflections on my profession; for Solomon plainly says, 'Do not despise a thief'". He followed this up by pointing out how useless was any debate, because the victor would inevitably be the one holding a gun. The terrified old Puritan found this difficult to deny, and handed over thirty pieces of gold. The pair parted—but even then Hind coolly returned with a scriptural reason as to why he should further relieve the astonished preacher of his coat as well.

Another notable regicide robbed by Hind was Major-General Thomas Harrison. The robbery took place on the Bath Road at Maidenhead Thicket, and a hue and cry was immediately raised. Shortly afterwards, whilst taking refreshment at a nearby inn, Hind was warned of the

Sensational tales about Hind were spread by pamphleteers to an increasingly literate population hungry for gossip

A contemporary engraving of Hind's attack on Thomas Harrison. Inset: Harrison, dandy and fanatic

impending danger. He immediately mounted and galloped off. Soon he heard a horseman riding at full speed behind him. Supposing this to be one of his pursuers, Hind turned in the saddle and shot the rider dead.

But Hind was mistaken. The dead man had not been chasing him. He was, George Sympson, a gentleman's servant, who had been riding fast simply because he had fallen behind his master. It was for this killing that Hind was later arraigned, rather than highway robbery.

Another story allows Hind to parade the requisite courtesy towards the fairer sex. Approaching a coach filled with gentlewomen, he explained pleasantly that it was purely to win the favour of a hard-hearted mistress that he "travelled the country". Touched by such knight-errantry, the ladies lamented that they had nothing with them with which to support him in his quest save only three bags each containing a thousand pounds

Hind was courteous to the ladies —but he still took their money

NO JEST Like a true jest:

Being a Compendious

RECORD

Of the

Merry Life, and Mad Exploits

OF

Capt. *JAMES HIND*

The Great Rober of *England*.

Together with the close of all at *Worcester*, where he was Drawn, Hang'd, and Quartered, for High-Treason against the Common-wealth: *Septemb.* 24. 1652.

London, Printed by *A. P.* for *T. Vere*, and are to be sold at his Shop, at the sign of the *Angel* without *Newgate*. 1674.

which, he would understand, they were holding on sacred trust as the dowry to be delivered to the betrothed of one of the party.

"My humble duty be presented to the knight," said James, "and be pleased to tell him that my name is Captain Hind; that out of mere necessity I have made bold to borrow part of what, for his sake, I wish were twice as much." At the name of Captain Hind the ladies realised they had been duped, and immediately surrendered the bag containing the thousand pounds. Graciously foregoing the other two bags of cash, the captain wished them all a good journey, and much joy to the bride.

When he was eventually brought to justice, Hind agreed that many of the stories about him stretched the truth but, he insisted, "some merry Pranks and Revels I have plaid, that I deny not".

In September 1652, James Hind's head was stuck on a pike on the Bridge Gate over the River Severn at Worcester. A week later it was spirited away.

James Hind was thirty-four when his head was stuck on a spike in Worcester

8
The child bride of Ditchley Park

IN FEBRUARY 1677 pretty Charlotte Fitzroy stood nervously at the altar in the Chapel Royal at Whitehall Palace. She was to be married to a newly-created earl with an estate at Ditchley near Enstone. And just over a year later Charlotte would be a mother. Nothing unusual there, one might think—except that the little bride was just twelve years old,

Charlotte Fitzroy in 1674, the year of her betrothal

Barbara Villiers, Lady Castlemaine

and within the year she would be a mother.

The circumstances were far from normal in another way too. Charlotte was the illegitimate daughter of King Charles II. Her mother was the King's mistress, Barbara Villiers, the infamous Lady Castlemaine.

Barbara Castlemaine was a bit of a handful. Voluptuous, with a mass of dark hair and heavy-lidded, violet eyes, she rampaged about Charles's Court, shouting the odds and spitefully flaunting her fertility over Charles's queen, the blameless and loyal—but barren—Catherine of Braganza. Indeed in 1662, instead of retiring discreetly to the country, Barbara chose to give birth to her second child at Hampton Court Palace while the King and Queen were honeymooning there.

Whitehall Palace at the time of Charlotte's marriage

Charlotte was born on 5th September 1664 at her mother's Whitehall Palace apartments. She was the eighth of a dozen illegitimate children acknowledged by the King. Happily, Charlotte did not share her mother's tempestuous nature. She was more like Charles: sweet-natured, fun-loving and affectionate. Father and daughter were very close, and it was said pointedly that Charlotte "rivalled her mother in beauty, but was far unlike her in every other respect".

Hardly surprisingly, therefore, there was considerable competition for Charlotte's hand in marriage. An alliance with a royal child, even an illegitimate one, was an attractive proposition. Engineered chiefly by the groom's grandmother the Countess of Rochester, a marriage contract between the King's bastard daughter and Edward Henry Lee was agreed in 1674. The couple were nine and eleven years old respectively.

Upon the betrothal, young Edward was created Earl of Lichfield.

Charlotte Fitzroy and her fiancé upon the occasion of their betrothal

They were married on 6th February 1677. And let us make no mistake. This was definitely not one of those royal marriages where children are formally married, but live apart until they reach a more appropriate age. The pair had already been betrothed for two and a half years by the time they married. Charlotte became pregnant within weeks, and gave birth to her first child in March 1678 at the age of thirteen. Even at the time, the tender ages of the young couple caused raised eyebrows.

Edward Lee of Ditchley: a father by the time he was fifteen years old

Henry and Charlotte spent their summers at Ditchley in Oxfordshire, the Lee family's country estate since 1580. Their London home was a property granted by the King to Sir Walter St John (Edward's great uncle), Sir Ralph Verney, Sir Richard Howe and John Cary on a ninety-nine year lease. Described as "all that piece… of Ground with the Buildings thereupon Within our Parke called St James Parke—bounded Eastward with the Buildings of the Cockpitt, Southward with the Wall

Charlotte was adored by her father the King, and also by her uncle, the future James II

The young couple's London home on the edge of Horse Guards Parade

of Hampden Garden, Northward one hundred and forty foote in length to the said Parke, Westward eighty five foote in length to the Parke." Today the property is the impressive building on Horse Guards Parade designed by Sir Christopher Wren and fronted by Downing Street.

Edward Lee has been described as a dedicated Tory and zealous follower of James II. He was Colonel of the first Regiment of Foot Guards in 1688, and served as Lord Lieutenant of Oxfordshire from 1687 to 1689. As for Charlotte, unlike the references to her mother Lady Castlemaine, those to her are all favourable. She was the only one of her mother's three daughters not to cause a scandal.

After such an early start, Charlotte presented her husband with no fewer than eighteen children. Five sons predeceased Edward and Charlotte, aged respectively five months, thirty-two, thirty, another infant, and twenty. Even the well-fed and cosseted aristocracy were not protected from the appalling toll which disease could take.

The house that we see today at Ditchley Park was built in 1722 by

Edward and Charlotte's sixth son George, second Earl of Lichfield. On George's death in 1743, the title passed to his son George Henry Lee, third Earl, who represented Oxfordshire in the House of Commons.

The third Earl died childless in 1772 and was succeeded by his uncle Robert, Charlotte's youngest son (another six boys had died in the meantime). Along with his father and nephew, Robert greatly beautified the house and park at Ditchley.

The little child-bride Charlotte died aged fifty-four. Her forty-two year-long marriage to Edward was apparently a happy one. The inscription on their monument in Spelsbury church tells us that: "It was Justly Observed That at their Marriage They were The most Gracefull Bridegroom and most Beautyfull Bride, And that till Death They remain'd The most Constant Husband and Wife."

Ditchley Park today: now a conference centre promoting international relations

But of all those eighteen babies that Charlotte bore, none could save the Lichfield title for the Lee family. For the fourth Earl Robert was childless, so his death while out hunting one day in 1776 was the end of the Lichfield line. The Earl of Lichfield so familiar to us today, photographer Patrick Lichfield, descended from a later creation of the title for the Anson family of Shugborough Hall in Staffordshire in 1831.

Charlotte was greatly respected and admired by her extended family

9
The miser of Marcham Park

LIEUTENANT COLONEL Richard Timms of the second Troop of Horse Guards knocked loudly on the door of an empty house in Great Marlborough Street in London one day in the late eighteenth century. No answer. He called out; still no answer. The colonel summoned assistance from a blacksmith so that he might enter the house through the stables. Hearing faint groans issuing from the first floor, the colonel climbed the stairs. There, on a simple pallet-bed, he found an old man, starved and near to death. But the old man was not some tramp of the district. He was the colonel's uncle, and he was one of the richest men in the land.

Marcham Park, now "Denman": heavily remodelled in 1820

John Meggot Elwes of Marcham Park inherited three enormous fortunes: the first from his father who died in 1718 when John was just four years old, the second from his mother in 1756 worth the equivalent today of eight million pounds and which included the Marcham Park estate, and a third in 1763 from his uncle, worth eighteen million pounds, inherited just before Elwes reached the age of fifty. So how had such a man come to be in an empty house in Soho, near to death from lack of food?

John Elwes was a miser. It had become his custom when visiting London to move between his many rental properties there, setting up home with just his housekeeper, a table and a couple of chairs in whichever house was vacant at the time. He existed on the merest scraps of food, often putrid, and forced his servants to do the same. In fact, on searching the house in Great Marlborough Street, Colonel Timms found the housekeeper lying dead on a rug in the attic, having apparently starved or frozen to death—or both—a couple of days before.

As a young man, Elwes had a reputation as quite the man-about-town, mixing with a fast set. He certainly developed a taste for gambling, at which he lost vast quantities of money. But he learned miserliness at the knee of his mean uncle Sir Harvey Elwes. Keen to ingratiate himself

As a young man, Elwes was an enthusiastic gambler

with rich uncle Harvey, John Elwes cast off his fine clothes before a visit and appeared in rags. He would also enjoy a hearty meal at the local inn beforehand, so that he might impress his uncle by eating sparingly in his presence. Sir Harvey bequeathed his entire fortune to his nephew, and the possession of so much money seemed to bring out in Sir John inclinations of his own towards extreme frugality.

Servants in the Elwes household were expected to lead as Spartan a life as their master. The huntsman was in reality obliged to serve as a

Elwes did not lack a sense of humour: when a friend wounded him on the cheek while they were out shooting, Elwes merely congratulated the embarrassed gentleman, saying that he always knew the man would hit something eventually

One thing Elwes did not stint on was his stable of hunters

man-of-all-work. He rose at four, milked the cows, served his master's breakfast, and then saddled up the horses and let out the hounds for the hunt to make off across the fields for the day. On returning, he would rub down the horses, run to the house to serve dinner, dash back out to the stables to feed the horses, and then relax during the evening by milking the cows again, feeding the hounds, and littering down eight horses for the night. John Elwes considered this human dynamo an "idle dog".

Elwes never married, but he did have two sons by Elizabeth Moren, his housekeeper at Marcham Park. He doted on the boys, but he refused to pay to have them educated, opining that "putting things into people's heads was the surest way to take money out of their pockets".

As Elwes's wealth expanded, so did the number of people offering to relieve him of it. He fell prey to the clumsiest of scams and the most unrealistic visions of distant property deals in America, annuities on phantom lives that would never mature, or bonds drawn on peers who had long since been divested of all their property.

On the other hand, it must be added that Elwes had a firm rule about never approaching a gentleman to pay back a debt. Hence he dealt out loans that would never be repaid, like the seven thousand pounds he advanced of his own volition to Lord Abingdon on a bet that Lord A very much wished to make at Newmarket. It is reckoned that, during his lifetime, Elwes lost altogether something in the order of one hundred and fifty thousand pounds (half a million pounds today) in unrecovered loans and unwise investments.

Fires were lit only sparingly at Marcham Park, and candles not at all if there was already a fire to see by. Repairs were never carried out, and once when Colonel Timms stayed with his uncle, he was awoken by the rain coming in through the roof. It has been suggested that Elwes was the model for Dickens's character Scrooge.

But if it were his time that was called upon and not his purse, Elwes could display astonishing generosity. Two elderly spinsters in the Mar-

Dickens is thought to have based the fictional character Scrooge on John Elwes

After cutting both legs badly, Elwes paid the apothecary to treat only one, betting him his fee that the leg he treated himself would heal first. Elwes won the bet

Portman Square: Elwes financed the redevelopment of much of Georgian London

cham area who somehow fell foul of their local church minister were threatened with excommunication the very next day. Upon learning of the defenceless ladies' plight, Elwes—the man who pulled down crows' nests to use the twigs on his fire and wore a wig discarded by a tramp in a lane—had his horse saddled up and rode sixty miles overnight to London to have the dreadful sentence lifted.

Besides serving as a Member of Parliament, Elwes's accomplishments included financing the construction of a significant amount of Georgian London including Portman Place, Portman Square, and parts of Oxford Circus, Piccadilly, Baker Street and Marylebone.

In his twilight days, Elwes grew feverish, stashing packets of money hither and thither about the house, and constantly returning to check that they were still there. He would struggle with imaginary intruders in the night, crying out: "I will keep my money! I will! Don't rob me! Oh, don't!" When asked who he was fighting with, Elwes would reply: "Sir, I beg your pardon, my name is Elwes, I have been unfortunate enough to be robbed in this house, which I believe is mine, of all the money I have in the world of five guineas and a half, and half a crown."

The family doctor pronounced that, but for his continual anxiety about money, Elwes might have lived twenty years longer. And the barrister called upon to draw up the will was forced to do so by firelight in order to save the cost of a candle.

Elwes died in his bed on 26th November 1789 with his tattered shoes on his feet, an old torn hat on his head, and a stick in his hand—his customary nightwear. Having lived on only fifty pounds a year, Elwes left five hundred thousand pounds (approximately twenty-eight million pounds today) to his beloved, illegitimate sons.

His great friend and biographer Edward Topham summed up Elwes as follows: "His public character lives after him pure and without stain. In private life, he was chiefly an enemy to himself. To others, he lent much; to himself, he denied everything. But in the pursuit of his property, or in the recovery of it, I have it not in my remembrance one unkind thing that ever was done by him."

10
The smooth operator of Shirburn Castle

WHEN RICHARD PARKER, ninth Earl of Macclesfield, learned in 2003 that he was to be evicted by other family members from dreamy Shirburn Castle near Watlington, his wife announced crisply to a journalist that: "If they [other family members] do move in, they will be taking on a shell. The contents belong to my husband." Picky modern taxpayers might be forgiven a slight splutter.

And what contents they were. Having already sold the papers of Isaac Newton to Cambridge University for over six million pounds, Lord

Shirburn Castle: built in 1377 for Warin de Lisle

Macclesfield anticipated netting a further twenty million pounds or so from the remaining treasures in the library, plus masterpieces including a Hogarth and a Stubbs. "There is no dispute that the contents of fourteenth-century Shirburn Castle belong one hundred per cent to the earl," trumpeted the *London Evening Standard*.

But Shirburn Castle and it dazzling contents were purchased by Lord Macclesfield's ancestor, the first earl, with funds which were—how can one put it politely?—misappropriated. Built in 1378, its four corner

Thomas Parker: he was described as having a "craving nature"

towers and surrounding moat make Shirburn perhaps the quintessential castle. It was an extraordinary purchase for a grammar school boy with no aristocratic blood.

For the first earl of Macclesfield was born plain Thomas Parker in Leek in 1667, the son of a modest Staffordshire attorney. His parents had eloped, with the consequent loss of his mother's dowry, and his father's legal practice seems to have been less than successful. All in all, money was scarce while Thomas was growing up.

By the time Thomas was seventeen years old, it was clear that he showed promise. His father approached the distinguished retired Parliamentarian soldier Colonel Robert Venables to ask for funds to send young Thomas to university. Parker claimed that he had been "importuned by some persons of quality and others who are able to judge of a lad's capacity for learning to send my son to the university".

The request was refused, leading Thomas's father to report that "my son's teeth are set on edge with the sour grapes which his parents have eaten…" Such straitened circumstances in early life may explain Thomas's apparent greed and obsession with money later on.

Eventually Thomas entered Trinity College, Cambridge, in October 1685. Although he took no degree, he was called to the bar in 1694. In 1705 he was created a bencher of the Middle Temple, and also made a QC. He became a rich and powerful lawyer, and threw himself into local politics as a confirmed Whig.

Like many provincial squires, Thomas became an MP and was knighted in 1705. His move to London helped his legal career to prosper, and he appeared frequently as counsel before the House of Lords. His only other connection with the aristocracy was that his wife Jennetta, whom he married in 1691, had a sister who was the wife a baronet.

He was made a Privy Counsellor in 1710, and his interest in science led him to be elected a Fellow of the Royal Society in 1713, and to acquire the papers of Isaac Newton. It was around this time that he

A patron of the sciences, Thomas acted as a pall-bearer at the funeral of Isaac Newton in March 1727

became a great book collector. One of his most precious acquisitions was a lavishly illuminated book of psalms produced in East Anglia in the early 1300s. It became known as the *Macclesfield Psalter* (below).

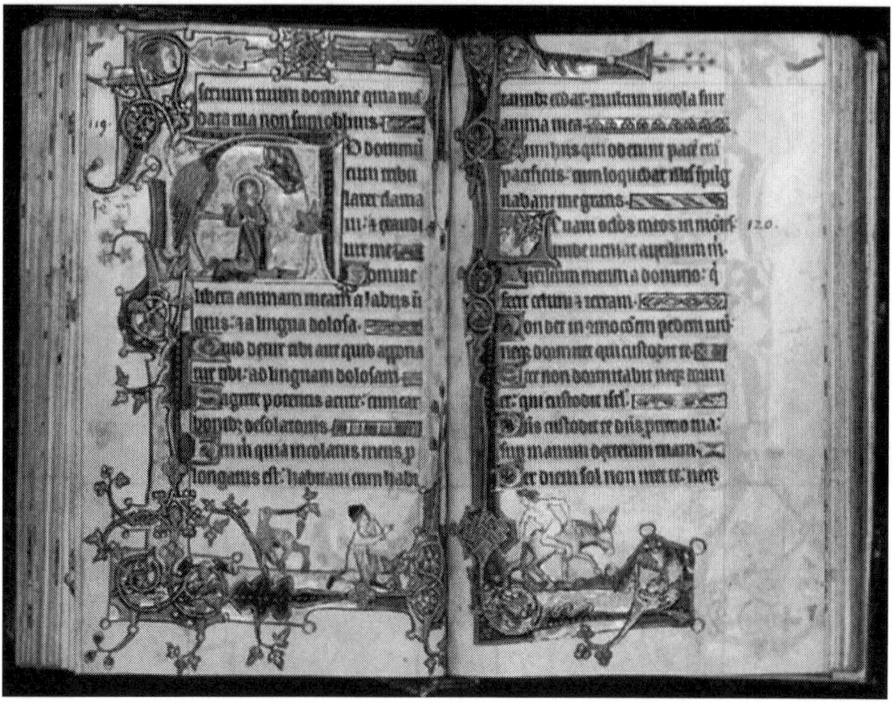

Thomas became a favourite of Queen Anne's successor George I

When Queen Anne died in 1714 her successor George I was still in Hanover, so Thomas was made one of seven regents until the new king could take over. The grammar school boy from Leek jointly ruled the realm for six weeks. And it was shortly after this, in 1716, that Thomas suddenly found himself with the funds not just to buy Shirburn Castle for eighteen thousand three hundred and fifty pounds, but also to make considerable alterations to the buildings and the park. He rebuilt the south and east ranges, constructed the fine staircase in the north-east corner, and remodelled the north and west ranges. As he was also accumulating that large collection of books for which the present earl is so grateful, Thomas was probably responsible for the famous two-roomed library as well.

A favourite of the new king, Thomas became Lord Chancellor in 1718 with a Treasury pension for life. But rumours were abroad that this was not enough for Thomas, and that he was taking massive backhanders. Prime Minister Robert Walpole—whose own reputation was far from spotless—was jealous of Thomas's personal influence with the king. He saw his chance and took advantage of the whispers to appoint a committee of the Privy Council to investigate the matter.

Twenty-one articles of impeachment condemned Thomas Parker to the Tower of London

Among the long list of charges, Thomas was accused of dealing in masterships in Chancery and of receiving bribes for agreeing to the sale and transfer of offices. Walpole's friend Sir George Oxenden moved the impeachment, and Walpole's opponents William Pulteney and Sir William Wyndham, leader of the Tories, were Thomas's defenders. The trial took place in the House of Lords in 1725, and Thomas himself is said to have put up a spirited show.

But the verdict was unanimous. Thomas was found guilty of corruption and fined thirty thousand pounds. To compound his humiliation, the House of Lords also dismissed Thomas from the Privy Council, and while the fine remained unpaid, he was imprisoned in the Tower of London. He claimed that previous confiscations had left him without the resources to pay the fine.

In fact, he was saved by his friend King George I, who promised to defray Thomas's pension payments from the Treasury in discharge of the thirty thousand pounds fine. But after the king's death in 1727, Walpole banned any further payments from the Treasury. Since few attorneys' sons lived in magnificent, moated castles stuffed to the gunwales with priceless treasures, it seems not entirely unreasonable to speculate that these might have been paid for from Thomas's ill-gotten gains. He was lucky that his castle and collections were not seized to pay off his fine.

Thomas lived in splendour for the rest of his days at beautiful Shirburn Castle surrounded by all those sumptuous goodies and, at his death in 1732, he was buried in the church there. His wife Jennetta survived him by only one year, and is buried alongside him.

Following the family row of the twenty-first century, Thomas's descendant the ninth Earl has moved to another house on the estate, and the castle is now empty of its treasures and remains unoccupied and unused.

The ninth Earl (right) was forced out of his home in 2004

11
The hell-raiser of All Souls' College

RESIDING UNTIL Judgment Day in a vault in the chapel of All Souls' College is the body of a celebrated judge connected with some of the most venerable institutions in the land. Robert Vansittart matriculated from Trinity College in 1745; he became a member of the Inner Temple in 1753; and he was elected a fellow of All Souls' College in 1757. During the 1760s he served as a circuit-judge for Maidenhead, Newbury, and Windsor, and finally in 1767 he arrived at the peak of his profession when he was appointed Regius Professor of Civil Law in the University of Oxford. Unknown to the ordinary folk whose fates he decided in court, however, Vansittart was at the very same time a member of another exclusive institution: the Hellfire Club.

The entrance to the Hellfire Club

Vansittart's friend Sir Francis Dashwood had the caves extended to house club meetings

This was a name used by several eighteenth-century clubs for high society rakes, but it usually refers to the one Vansittart belonged to, which met in a network of caves underneath West Wycombe Park in Berkshire. The Order of the Friars of St Francis of Wycombe, as the club was originally known, was the brainchild of Vansittart's friend Sir Francis Dashwood. While on the Grand Tour as a young man, Sir Francis had developed an acute dislike of the Catholic church, and the revelries he masterminded back home at the Hellfire Club took a deliberate swipe at Rome's rituals and representatives.

Sir Frances Dashwood: the Elton John of his day

Follies and grottoes in the Gothic style were fashionable at the time, and Dashwood extended a series of chalk mines under his estate to serve as a discreet venue for racy parties. A dramatic flint façade with a vaulted window formed the entrance to the caves. Above it was displayed the club motto, "*Libertati Amicatiae que S*" ("Sacred to liberty and friendship"). High walls on either side were studded with niches for displaying representations of the Order's particular deities, Bacchus and Venus. The walls bounded a large open courtyard in between. From the house across the valley this was all, of course, intended to resemble a spookily tumbledown Gothic church.

Deep, winding passages extended underground for over a quarter of a mile. As well as a series of smaller chambers, there was a large, vaulted banqueting hall. The very deepest chamber, the so-called Inner Temple, lay some three hundred feet directly beneath St Lawrence's church, juxtaposing Heaven and Hell on the same site. Everywhere were to be seen pagan and satanic symbols and figures of a distinctly saucy nature.

The "monks" called themselves Franciscans to reflect Dashwood's Christian name, and they amused themselves with rude parodies of Franciscan rites, drunken feasting and riotous wenching. Meetings

The banqueting hall and (above) some of the lurid carvings decorating the caves and tunnels

A scene from "The Rake's Progress" by William Hogarth, an occasional guest at the club

occurred twice a year, with an AGM lasting a week or more. Members addressed each other as "Brother" and the leader as "Abbot". The Abbot was elected annually and took up office at the beginning of October.

Chapter meetings are described in a book of 1779: "They always meet in one general sett at meals, when, for the improvement of mirth, pleasantry, and gaiety, every member is allowed to introduce a Lady of cheerful lively disposition, to improve the general hilarity. [These ladies, by the way, were known as 'nuns'.] No vows of celibacy were required either by the ladies or the 'monks', the former considering themselves as the lawful wives of the brethren during their stay within the monastic walls; every monk being religiously scrupulous not to infringe upon the nuptial alliance of any other Brother."

After dinner, the twelve core members and the Abbot repaired to the Inner Temple where a mock religious ceremony took place. Members supposedly wore a uniform of white trousers, jacket and cap, while the Abbot sported a red ensemble in the same style. Later tales of serious

The Earl of Sandwich (left) fell out with radical MP John Wilkes (right)

devil-worship and black magic were probably the fruits of fevered Victorian imagination.

To this day the identities of all the members of the Hellfire Club remain obscure. But as Sir Francis's number one partner-in-crime, John Montagu, fourth Earl of Sandwich, must be included. He was First Lord of the Admiralty, but is perhaps best known for the claim that he invented the sandwich as a snack which might conveniently be consumed without the diner leaving the gambling table.

Not all was comradely loyalty at the Hellfire Club, however, and Sandwich took against his fellow monk, radical MP John Wilkes. A prank by Wilkes involved the release without warning of a baboon dressed in a cape and horns. The terrified creature leapt onto the shoulders of an equally terrified Earl of Sandwich, who immediately begged what he believed to be Satan himself to spare him on the grounds that most of the escapades of which he had boasted over the years had actually been made up.

In revenge for this humiliating episode, Sandwich took a leading part in the successful prosecution of Wilkes for libel. When Sandwich announced to Wilkes that he would either die on the gallows or of the

Party-free zone: Vansittart's final resting place

pox, Wilkes replied without hesitation: "That must depend on whether I embrace your lordship's principles or your mistress."

A likely visitor to the club was Vansittart's friend Dr Samuel Johnson, who held Vansittart in great affection. In a moment of playfulness during a visit to Oxford in 1759, the fifty year-old, comfortably-built Dr Johnson proposed that together the pair should scale the walls of All Souls' for a lark. On another occasion, while Vansittart was relating a lengthy story of a flea, an exasperated Johnson eventually spluttered: "It is a pity, sir, that you have not seen a lion; for a flea has taken you such a time that a lion must have served you for a twelve-month!" Another literary friend, Goethe, based a character in a play on Vansittart.

By the mid-1770s the Hellfire members were getting old and the club was on the wane. An inventory dated 15th October 1774 listed the contents of the cellar: "Lisbon [sherry], rum, port, hock, claret and Dorchester beer, as well as 29 pewter plates, 27 knives and 29 forks, 24 wine glasses and—[rather sweetly]—some teacups and saucers." All other club records were burned. Vansittart himself died at Oxford, unmarried and aged sixty-one, on 31st January 1789. He lies quietly to this day in his vault in the chapel at All Souls' College.

Vansittart's literary friends: Dr Samuel Johnson (left) and the German poet Goethe

12
The minx of Middleton Park

IT WOULD BE UNFAIR to brand Frances Villiers of Middleton Park near Middleton Stoney a tart. After all, Lady Jersey didn't sleep with her friends' husbands for personal gain. She did it just for the heck of it. Having worked her way through society, she eventually became the mistress of the Prince of Wales, the future Prince Regent. She was forty years old and a grandmother.

Of course, Frances had an unfortunate start in life. Her father Philip Twysden was shot while attempting to hold up a stagecoach on Hounslow Heath. Embarrassing enough, you might think, but her father was

High society hold-up: Twysden tried moonlighting as a highwayman

George Bussy Villiers, fourth Earl of Jersey: he married Frances Twysden in London in March 1770 when he was thirty-four and Frances was just seventeen

also a bishop. Having frittered away the family fortune, he had fixed upon this desperate course. The bishop died the day after the robbery, and Frances was born three months later in February 1753. Just after her seventeenth birthday in 1770, Frances married the thirty-four year-old Earl of Jersey, George Villiers. The couple had ten children, though it seems entirely possible that they may not all have borne a close resemblance to the Earl. For Frances's lovers included Frederick Howard, fifth Earl of

A selection of Frances's conquests: the Earl of Carlisle, his son Lord Morpeth…

… William Fawkener, and the Duke of Devonshire

Carlisle; the Earl's son Lord Morpeth; diplomat and clerk to the Privy Council William Augustus Fawkener; and the husband of Frances's friend Georgiana, William Cavendish, fifth Duke of Devonshire.

Frances was said to embody "a heady mix of charm, beauty, and sarcasm". She was described in the journal of Mary Frampton as "a clever, unprincipled, but beautiful and fascinating woman, though with scarcely any retrieving really good quality". And Harriet, Lady Bessborough, claimed that Lady Jersey was never happy unless she had "a rival to trouble and torment".

All of these traits, good and bad, were mobilised when Frances became mistress of the Prince of Wales in 1793. The Prince had already been lusting after Frances for several years, during which time he had contracted an invalid marriage with his primary mistress, the Catholic Maria Fitzherbert. Determined to establish her own supremacy and compromise Mrs Fitzherbert's position into the bargain, Frances came up with a wheeze. She would urge the Prince to make a legal marriage with a woman she could control.

Princess Caroline of Brunswick could never hope to compete with the dazzling charms of Lady Jersey. Vulgar, plain, and—to be perfectly frank—a bit whiffy, poor Caroline had to endure the humiliation of Lady Jersey's appointment as Lady of the Royal Bedchamber. And Frances did nothing to alleviate the Princess's suffering, allowing her talent for spite and cruelty free rein. She paraded around London in the Prince's coach, escorted by the Prince's liveried servants just as if she were the Princess of Wales herself.

When Caroline begged her husband to remove Frances from her household, Lady Jersey decided to ramp things up a bit. Exploiting her privileged access to Caroline's private apartments, naughty Frances smuggled out some of the Princess's letters complaining about the Prince. Somehow the letters then found their way into the hands of

Caroline of Brunswick: she lived apart from her husband throughout their twenty-five-year marriage

the Prince's mother, Queen Charlotte. All this simply served further to endear Caroline to a sympathetic public who already appreciated her unstuffy manner and friendly nature, and abhorred the Prince of Wales's shabby treatment of her. He restricted her freedom to travel and limited her access to her only daughter, Princess Charlotte. Caroline was

Frances Villiers: at first she enjoyed the favour of the Prince of Wales's mother Queen Charlotte

Cartoonists were ruthless in their treatment of Frances and the Prince

cheered whenever she appeared in public; the Prince and Lady Jersey were booed—and worse. Rotting vegetables were among the missiles aimed at the Prince—unthinkable today. In Brighton in 1796 Frances was burned in effigy. And when her London house was pelted with stones, she became genuinely frightened even within her own home.

Former friends of her own class began to drop her too. Famously, upon arrival at the Duchess of Gordon's ball, she received no greeting. When she approached people in an attempt to join the party, they simply turned away. She was shunned by society, and her time at the top was running out.

In June 1796 she resigned from her post as Lady of the Bedchamber, and over the next few years she lost her grip on power over the Prince's household. He had tired of Lady Jersey, and turned his wandering eye elsewhere. As you may imagine, Frances was not prepared to go quietly. When her husband the Earl of Jersey was threatened with debtor's prison, she hounded the Prince of Wales until he paid what was owed

Irresistible: the Prince of Wales, future Prince Regent and King George IV

to the Earl so that he might clear his debts.

She worked hard to ensure that her own ruined reputation did not scupper the chances of her beloved children making good marriages. And in spite of her disgraceful behaviour, the long-suffering Earl stood by her to the end. To the considerable surprise of society, Frances was devastated at the Earl's death in 1805. She was also pretty miffed at the consequent curtailment of her own lifestyle, and badgered the Prince of Wales into paying her a pension. Even so, she was a stranger to financial prudence, and had regularly to be bailed out by her son, the fifth Earl of Jersey.

Frances sallied on causing trouble for everyone around her until July 1821, when she died four days after the Prince of Wales's coronation as George IV. She was sixty-eight.

Middleton Park as Frances would have known it. The present house was built in the 1930s

13
The secret lovers of Buscot Park

THIRD TIME LUCKY, or so they say. Edward Loveden of Buscot Park near Faringdon must have been delighted with his new bride—a lovely young woman half his age at twenty-one. By the time he was thirty-eight he had been widowed twice, and he had considered the matter for a full six years before taking the plunge yet again in 1794.

Anne Lintall, daughter of Thomas Lintall of modest little Norbiton Hall in Surrey, was doubtless amazed at her good fortune when she first set eyes upon her palatial marital home at Buscot Park. Under con-

Buscot Park: two Mrs Lovedens had already presided here before young Anne Lintall arrived

struction since 1780, the neo-classical house and park were now largely complete, though Edward continued to fiddle with the design of the gardens for years.

But settling in to a life with a husband constantly away attending to his duties as an MP, a lieutenant colonel of the Berkshire militia, and a Fellow of the Royal Society wasn't easy for young Anne. And carving out a place for herself in a household where her step-children were only a few years younger than herself was perhaps a challenge too.

Edward Loveden: he changed his name from Townsend when he inherited the Loveden estate from his great-uncle

Norbiton Hall: Anne was married from the Lintall family's home in Kingston-upon-Thames

Some ten years into the childless marriage, the servants began to notice an attachment forming between their mistress and a handsome young family friend. Temptation had presented itself in the dashing form of known-ladies'-man Thomas ("Tom") Raymond Barker of Fairford Park in Gloucestershire. Barker was several years Anne's junior, a Fellow of Merton College, Oxford. He was the younger son of an old friend of Edward's. Edward had treated the boy with great generosity and hospitality over the years, supporting him financially at Oxford, and allowing him frequently to stay overnight at Buscot when journeying between Fairford and the University. He even provided Tom with an expensive steed for the purpose.

During Edward's many absences Tom was a frequent visitor, walking arm-in-arm with Anne in the grounds at Buscot and remaining for long periods in seclusion with her in her private drawing-room—normally a no-go area for gentlemen. When Tom was a guest in the house, Anne ordered the servants to send callers away.

Damningly, the butler Hastings noticed that the pair would play footsie under the breakfast table in what he later called "a very peculiar and indecent fashion".

By 1807 Edward began to suspect his wife, but his friend Francis Knight advised him that it would be unwise to make a fuss unless he had positive evidence of Anne's faithlessness. Barker was known for his skirt-chasing, Knight reasoned, and this was probably just another of his crass flirtations.

Meanwhile, the servants were still alive to each and every occasion upon which Anne would emerge from an encounter with Barker, looking flustered and dishevelled. During a trip to London Anne picked up Tom in her carriage and, contrary to her usual custom, kept the blinds down in spite of stifling weather. After the carriage had driven about a bit, Anne emerged looked "much heated and red" and with her hair in a mess.

On another occasion, the lovers came close to being discovered *in flagrante* in the greenhouse at Buscot. A further close shave occurred

Fairford Park: family home of Anne's lover Tom Barker

when the cook searched high and low to ask Anne's advice on preparing a particularly delicate dish. At last Anne staggered out of the dining room with her skirts hitched round her legs. The cumulative effect of such tales from the servants was by now too much. Edward Loveden forbade Tom once and for all from entering the house and grounds at Buscot Park.

But he did come back, and the servants were by now on high alert. Prompted by Anne's surreptitious oiling of the locks to her rooms, they mounted a vigil one night in August 1808 when Edward was away in Abingdon. Outside in the dark, Hastings confronted Tom Barker with a loaded pistol as he jumped from the roof of the privy.

A discussion between the two men followed during which Hastings claims he offered to keep the incident quiet if Barker solemnly undertook never to visit Buscot again. A cynic might speculate that, as well as wishing to preserve his master from the upset and humiliation that would inevitably result from disclosure, Hastings may well have spotted a nice little earner.

Barker now stayed away, and Anne began to write desperate letters, one of which, in particular, would come back to haunt her. By the following spring she could bear the separation no longer, and when Edward was again away, this time visiting his son Pryse Loveden Pryse in Woodstock, she admitted Tom to the house. Something of a farce ensued. Suspecting the presence of Barker in the master's study, Hastings ordered the under-butler to climb onto a stool teetering on the windowsill outside in order to peer in. From this somewhat undignified position, the under-butler was able to confirm that, shrinking against the inside wall below, was Tom Barker.

In the ensuing court proceedings, and probably to the chagrin of both sides, a letter from Anne was read out for all to hear providing Barker with a sort of timetable specifying the weeks when she might best avoid conceiving. With such damning evidence, it looked as if Edward would

No winners: a cringe-making letter from Anne advising her lover of the timing of her monthly cycle was read out in court

get his divorce, but when he was ordered to pay Anne alimony of four hundred pounds a year, he furiously dropped the case. So not only had he openly ejected Anne from his household and allowed the public revelation of the embarrassing letter concerning her monthly cycle, but now he had also deprived Anne and Barker of the chance to marry. Furthermore, he left his wife with only her pin money to live on—perhaps around a hundred pounds a year. It was Edward Loveden's final revenge.

But, as so often in such cases, the wronged party turned out to be the biggest loser. He suffered public ridicule as the cuckolded old fool whose young wife had given herself with enthusiasm to a younger man. Loveden retired from most of his public duties.

Barker jumped from his academic position before he was pushed, and acquired a handsome three hundred-acre farm in Hambleden, Buckinghamshire, where he lived with Anne in great contentment. In spite of his colourful history he served as a local magistrate and, three years after Anne's death in 1821, he married at last.

14
The hero of Stratton Audley

BURIED IN the family vault at Stratton Audley, just about as far from the sea as it is possible to get in England, lies Admiral Sir John Borlase Warren, Knight Grand Cross of the Bath, Knight Grand Cross of Hanover, Privy Counsellor, and Member of Parliament. But never mind this catalogue of distinction. Pet-owners might secretly view Warren's greatest achievement as his pivotal contribution in righting a wrong concerning a scandalous case of celebrity dognapping in 1811.

Warren's naval career had at first been intermingled with his academic

Stratton Audley Manor: originally sixteenth century, but much altered in later years

one. Having had been admitted to Emmanuel College, Cambridge at the age of sixteen, Warren was then entered as an able seaman on the books of the *Marlborough* at eighteen. At twenty-one he was elected MP for Marlow in Buckinghamshire, and at twenty-two he assumed the baronetcy that had been extinct since the death of his great-grandfather.

Warren was known in his early years as something of a dandy. Like many young bucks of the time, he was a heavy gambler and he amused himself by purchasing a yacht together with a convenient mooring for

Sir John Borlase Warren: he was actually born in Nottinghamshire; Stratton Audley came to the Warren family by marriage in around 1700

sailing it in the Bristol Channel in the form of Lundy Island. He was considered a dashing and elegant officer, though perhaps not in the first rank tactically. Indeed, there was a suspicion that he was rather too interested in the prize money earned by taking enemy ships, especially when he employed a secretary devoted entirely to ensuring that he received every penny to which he was entitled—which was many.

He was commander-in-chief on the Royal Navy's North American station at Halifax, Nova Scotia, from 1807 to 1810 when he became an admiral. He was again commander-in-chief on this station from 1813 to 1814, and this was when he became involved in the celebrated case of brave little Pandour.

Pandour was a terrier named for his master Captain John Shortland's first ever command, the troopship *Pandour*. Quite when the canine Pandour joined Shortland's crew is unclear, but he was definitely on duty exactly when a dog is at his best.

In September 1809 Shortland was captain of the *Junon* when she sailed for the West Indies. On 13th December *Junon* fell in with four large frigates sailing under Spanish colours. The frigates appeared able to decipher *Junon*'s coded signals, so Shortland assumed they were friendly and stood towards them to gain intelligence of the enemy. But, when the *Junon* was well within gunshot, the other ship lowered the Spanish colours,

Captain John Shortland, Pandour's heroic master

Shortland was hit by "langridge" shot, a type of case shot used against men and rigging

hoisted French, and poured broadsides into *Junon*. Notwithstanding the odds against him, Shortland defended his ship with the utmost gallantry until he was personally peppered with shot.

It was said at the time that Shortland received the greatest number of serious wounds ever known in one action. He was wounded in both legs, and sustained an injury in his side; his left arm and hand were shattered to pieces, and all his knuckles were broken. His head was the only part uninjured. He was carried below, severely maimed. His right leg

A night-time engagement: a painting thought to depict the attack on the Junon. *Inset: artist's impression of Pandour, who remained steadfast throughout*

was amputated above the knee, as well as a finger, and grape shot was extracted from his hand. And throughout this succession of horrors, the valiant Pandour remained at his master's side.

Shortland's sufferings were made much worse by the fact that he had to be moved several times. First he was with great difficulty conveyed across a very heavy sea from the *Junon* to one of the French frigates. Then the *Junon*, which had lost ninety men killed and wounded, was boarded and captured. But she was found by the French to be such a complete wreck that she was cleared out and set on fire off Guadeloupe.

At last, aboard the French frigate Shortland found some respite in the captain's cabin. Unfortunately, it was to be only temporary. When the call rang out that an English frigate was in sight, the ship was cleared for action and poor Captain Shortland was picked up and shifted again, this time into the peace and quiet of the gun-room. Intelligence then arrived that several English vessels were blocking the entrance to the French-held harbour of Basseterre, meaning that the frigate would be unable to land there. Shortland's rescuers were forced to change course and run into a small creek.

There Captain Shortland was offloaded from the French frigate and plonked into a canoe for an agonising thirteen-mile trip under a scorching sun to the nearest hospital. For six weeks he lay, guarded, licked, and nuzzled by the steadfast Pandour. Eventually, exhausted by the loss of blood and worn out by extreme pain, Shortland died a national hero on 21st January 1810.

Pandour was brought back to England, but before he could make it home to the Shortland family he was stolen at the Elephant and Castle. Spirited away on board a ship, he arrived eventually at the Royal Navy's North American station in Halifax, Nova Scotia. By chance an injured member of the *Junon*'s crew, who had by then also returned to Halifax, recognised his old commander's dog. Pandour recognised the wounded sailor too, and immediately responded to his own name being called.

The Royal Navy's North American station at Halifax, Nova Scotia

The seaman demanded that the dog be given up, but the evil dognapper refused. And this is where Admiral Warren comes in. As commander-in-chief of the station, he was called upon to adjudicate between the two sailors. When he witnessed Pandour enthusiastically performing at the *Junon* sailor's command all the tricks that Shortland had taught him,

Pandour always recognised his Junon *shipmates*

Warren insisted that Pandour be given over to the sailor's care with a view to a return to the Shortland family.

And so it came to pass that, on 3rd March 1811, the much-travelled Pandour trotted inquisitively up a strangely familiar path to the front door of a smart house in London. The moment the door of the Shortland residence was opened, an excited Pandour recognised the family servant as yet another fellow veteran of the *Junon*, the very same man who had brought him up from a puppy. Unconfined joy was apparently expressed as only a terrier can.

Two years later, Warren's naval career was rounded off with his promotion from admiral of the blue to admiral of the white—just one rank below admiral of the red. He died suddenly in February 1822 at Greenwich Hospital while visiting the governor there.

Warren's two sons had predeceased him, so his estate was left to his daughter Frances. At her own death in 1837 it was reported that Frances's charitable donations amounted to over eight thousand pounds a year. It is rather pleasing to discover that much of Warren's enormous stash of prize money was eventually directed by Frances to the benefit of poor widows, orphans and the sick.

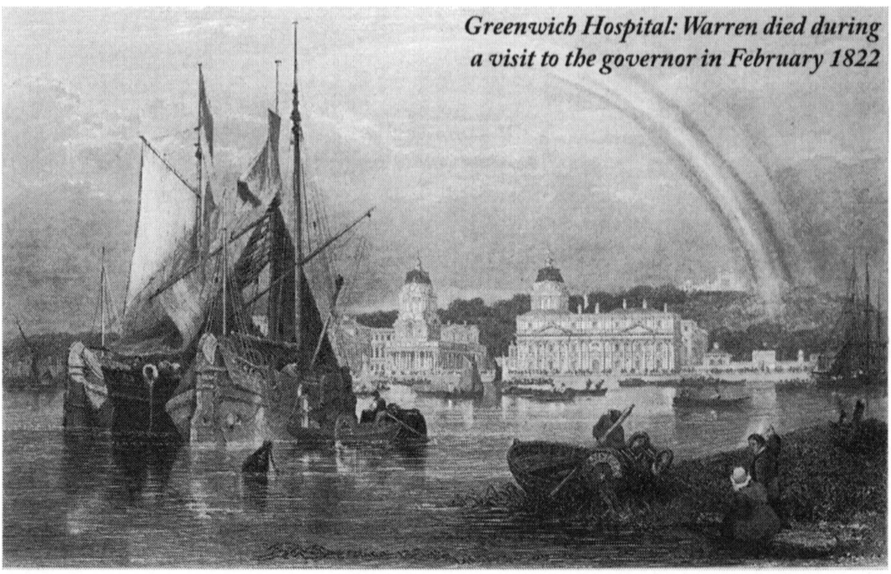

Greenwich Hospital: Warren died during a visit to the governor in February 1822

15
The burning lady of Woodstock House

LOGS CRACKLED in the fires, candles flickered and the musicians played up a storm at the Pryse family's New Year's Eve party in 1812. Pryse Loveden Pryse and his wife Harriet had decamped from their Oxfordshire home in Woodstock to Pryse's beloved Welsh estate of Plas Gogerddan in Cardiganshire for the celebrations. But the jollifications were to end in tragedy.

Pryse was the heir to the Buscot Park estate near Faringdon. Born Pryse Loveden in 1774, he adopted the surname Pryse in 1798 follow-

New Year's Eve 1812 was Harriet Pryse's last

ing the death of his maternal grandmother. From her he inherited thirty thousand acres in Wales which yielded an annual income of some six thousand pounds, as well as Woodstock House abutting the estate of the Duke of Marlborough at Blenheim.

In the same year he married widowed Harriet Agar, daughter of Viscount Ashbrook of Shellingford Manor. Two years Pryse's senior at twenty-six, Harriet was already touched by scandal. Her mother had been born a simple fisherman's daughter named Betty Ridge. Her father William Flower, second Viscount Ashbrook, met Betty when she was serving in her father's inn on an island in the river Thames at Northmoor. Against his family's wishes, the couple had married in 1766.

As a country squire broadly aligned to the Whigs, Pryse Loveden Pryse was happiest riding to hounds over his Welsh estates, but he dutifully set about remodelling the old-fashioned house in Woodstock which formed part of his inheritance from his grandmother as an Oxfordshire home for himself and his bride. High days and holidays, however, were spent in Cardiganshire.

Woodstock House: the Pryses' Oxfordshire home

Plas Gogerddan: scene of the mysterious fire

On that fateful night in 1812, Harriet Pryse did not retire to bed until the early hours of morning. The *Hull Packet* offered the official line: "As Mrs Pryse was preparing to go to bed between two and three o'clock on the morning of New Year's day, her night dress came in contact with a rush-light that was burning in the room, and was instantly in a blaze." The reader is reassured that, as a lady of breeding, Harriet did not allow such a circumstance to occasion undignified panic. "Notwithstanding

Rushlights remained in use in rural Wales long after they had fallen into disuse in England

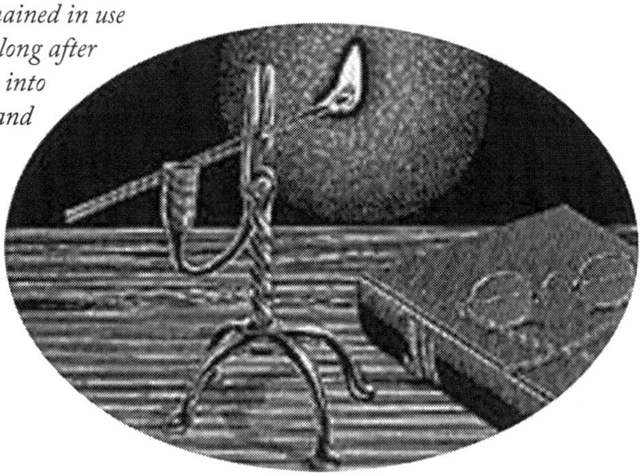

this alarming situation, Mrs Pryse had sufficient presence of mind to ring the bell; but, unfortunately, though almost immediate assistance was afforded, it had only the effect of preventing instant death." Harriet lingered in what must have been great agony for almost two weeks, dying eventually on 13th January.

For those close enough to Harriet to know that she had been bedridden for some years with a rheumatic condition, this official account did not add up. How could she attend festivities downstairs into the small hours, and then take herself off up a flight of stairs unassisted, and change into a nightgown with nobody in attendance? Rumours of a quite different sequence of events began to emerge. It was even whispered amongst the local people who knew Harriet well, served her daily, and were fond of her, that she had been murdered.

Throughout the holiday period the guests at Gogerddan had included the family of Pryse's friend Peter Cavallier of Guisborough in Yorkshire. The connection is a strange one. Descended from Huguenot refugees who fled from France at the beginning of the eighteenth century, Cavallier was a humble Yorkshire schoolmaster with a son who was a cabinet maker. He also had a daughter Jane, who, at the age of thirty, was running out of time to find a husband.

The alternative version of events suggested that, under cover of the noisy festivities below, one of the Cavalliers sneaked upstairs and tossed a lighted lamp on to Harriet's bed. Only those who have been felled by a serious rheumatic complaint throughout every joint will recognise that even reaching out to ring the bell under such circumstances may have been more than Harriet could manage. And her apparent lack of initiative in taking any other measures to save herself would also seem to be explained by an inability to move.

But why would the Cavalliers want to dispose of the wife of the staggeringly-rich Pryse Loveden Pryse? There is no evidence that Pryse had any wish to rid himself of his wife of fifteen years. Depicted on Harri-

Pryse Loveden Pryse of Woodstock showed genuine grief upon the grisly death of his wife Harriet

et's monument in the family church, the grieving Pryse rather touchingly covers his eyes with his hand in a simple gesture of manly despair. Indeed, the shock of his loss caused him to live for a while as a recluse, during which period his father Edward Loveden—always ready to leap to Pryse's vilification—feared that his son's behaviour was a manifestation of a latent mental instability thought to lurk in the Pryse family.

Rushing to Pryse's side to comfort him during this difficult time came Jane, the unmarried daughter of his friend Peter Cavallier. So comprehensively did she accomplish her mission of mercy that, by September 1814, she was expecting Pryse's child. Pryse married the heavily-pregnant Jane in April 1815 and she gave birth to a son four weeks later.

We shall probably never know what really happened to cause poor Harriet's death but, one way or

Edward Loveden of Buscot Park: Pryse's father doubted his son's sanity

Jane Cavallier's sons: Pryse, Edward and John

another, Jane Cavallier got her man. She presented Pryse with three sons, and the eldest, Pryse Pryse, inherited his father's enormous estates in Wales and Oxfordshire. Jane died at Gogerddan in 1846 aged sixty-four. Her husband died three years later aged seventy-five.

Jane Cavallier (left): triumphant, or just lucky?

16
The recluse of Blenheim Palace

IN AN OBSCURE CORNER of magnificent Blenheim Palace in the spring of 1840 an old man lived out his final days, surviving only on a post office pension. A venerable family retainer, perhaps, housed with casual good intentions, but now forgotten?

Actually, he was George Spencer-Churchill, fifth Duke of Marlborough, skulking out of sight in his ancestral home having fallen on extremely hard times. And it was entirely his own fault. A flamboyant society figure as a young man, George had blown the family fortune on a fantasy party-palace called Whiteknights.

Whiteknights at Earley near Reading

Whiteknights Park was adorned with all the fashionable garden features of the day

The Marquis of Blandford, as he then was, had settled his young family in an elegant Italianate mansion on the eighty-acre Whiteknights Park estate at Earley near Reading in 1798. George was a lover of fine things: clothes, art, gardens and—especially—books. Taking advantage of the apparently endless credit at that time extended to young aristocrats with expectations, he set about turning Whiteknights into a little Paradise for the connoisseur.

Having grown up at Blenheim, George had watched and learned while landscape designer Capability Brown transformed the park there for his father the fourth Duke. George laid out spectacular gardens at Whiteknights, full of all the features fashionable at the time. There was a lake with an iron bridge and a stone bridge, an ice-house and a Gothic chapel, believed by some to represent the ruins of the chapel of the sup-

Blenheim Palace: George had watched Capability Brown transform his childhood home

posed “White Knights”. A “chantilly garden” in the French style provided many seats—some critics sniped too many seats—set in ornate trellis pavilions.

George planted a vineyard, an extensive sheep walk, an elm grove, an oak grove, wych elms and cedars, and a wilderness. In 1817, the writer Mary Russell Mitford reported of her visit to the grounds that “there

Soon after succeeding to the dukedom in 1817, George added the illustrious name of his famous soldier-ancestor Churchill to his birth name Spencer

George's wife, Lady Susan Stewart

is a certain wood at Whiteknights, shut in with great boarded gates, which nobody is allowed to enter. It is a perfect Bluebeard's chamber; and, of course, all our pretty Fatimas would give their heads to get in." And to reinforce this clue as to the type of revelry that went on at Whiteknights when Lady Blandford was away, the housekeeper claimed that Mitford and her companion were the first two "modest ladies" she had ever admitted to the thrilling wood. Presumably paid enough to turn a blind eye to any aristocratic indiscretions were the members of the

The wilderness today and (inset) writer Mary Russell Mitford

Sturt's mistress, Fanny Krumpholtz

military band George hired to play to his guests.

The Marquis fancied himself something of a botanist, and he sent out around the globe for rare specimens for his gardens and hothouses. The lawns were studded with cast-iron and wooden baskets brimming with scarlet sage and begonias, at that time impossibly exotic. Even King George III supplied the exciting project with items from the royal gardens at Kew. One wall of dazzling white magnolia was said to measure one hundred and forty feet long and twenty feet high.

And this was just outside. Inside, Whiteknights House itself was so lavishly furnished that it was said to be fit for a king. A treasure trove of old masters encrusted the walls from the ornamental ceilings to the shining floors, and a thousand bottles of the finest wines and spirits jostled in the cellars. Unsurprisingly, therefore, Whiteknights became a favourite retreat for members of the royal family, though presumably those saucy Fatimas were kept away when Queen Charlotte was there.

Perhaps encouraged by the conspicuous spending at Whiteknights, one Sir Charles Sturt MP sued Blandford for criminal conversation with his wife, hoping to win twenty thousand pounds. Unfortunately for Sturt, it emerged at the trial that he himself had been keeping a mistress in the form of a Bohemian harp player and composer called Fanny Krumpholtz. Damages were awarded to Sturt—of one pound.

But George's greatest weakness was not wine or women, though he made sterling efforts in both areas. It was the Whiteknights library which was the chief glory among glories. George displayed exceptional

The Bedford Missal, now in the British Library

taste and discernment. In 1817 he acquired the exquisitely-illustrated Bedford Missal, commissioned by the Duke of Bedford in 1422 for Henry VI. It cost George six hundred and ninety-eight pounds. Even more expensive at two thousand, two hundred and sixty pounds—a record for a single book at the time—was the only perfect copy of a 1471 *Decameron* by Boccaccio purchased from the Duke of Roxburgh.

Sadly, the entire pleasure palace at Whiteknights was built on smoke and mirrors. In order to pay off the debts he had incurred, George took out yet more loans. But finally the merry-go-round of credit squealed to a halt; his creditors wanted their money back. In 1819 the house and all its contents were auctioned off—some at well under their proper value. The precious *Decameron* was knocked down to George's cousin Earl Spencer, who had bid against him at the original auction and lost, for nine hundred and eighteen pounds. Garden ornaments were removed, even the tiles on the roof were ripped off. No sign of the beautiful house now remains.

Having by now succeeded to the title of fifth Duke of Marlborough, George withdrew reluctantly to Blenheim Palace. Desperate measures were called on to keep the estate going, as revealed by the diarist Harriet Arbuthnot following a visit in 1824: "The family… is… gone sadly to decay,

Harriet Arbuthnot wrote of the sad state of affairs at the once-proud Blenheim Palace after a visit in 1824

Legal action was required to prevent George from selling off the timber in the park

and are but a disgrace to the illustrious name of Churchill, which they have chosen this moment to resume. The present Duke is overloaded with debt, is very little better than a common swindler, and lets everything about Blenheim. People may shoot and fish at so much per hour and it has required all the authority of a Court of Chancery to prevent his cutting down all the trees in the park." It is difficult to see what else George could do, however, apart from not blowing his fortune in the first place. The strict social taboo forbidding an aristocrat from earning his own living left him with few options.

George did manage to hold on to two of his treasures, however. Mysteriously concealed in the meagre baggage he took away from Whiteknights was that stunning Bedford Missal. Another treasure he held on to was Lady Mary Anne Sturt. The couple lived together for the rest of their lives, and George died with her close by him the day before his seventy-fourth birthday in 1840. His duchess Susan died aged 73 at her London home in Park Lane, Mayfair, in April 1841.

17
The blackmailer of Shipton Court

ON FRIDAY 30th June 1843 a grim scene unfolded in the parish church of St Mary the Virgin at Shipton-under-Wychwood. A coffin which had been interred three weeks earlier was exhumed and carried inside the church. There the lid was prised off, and those attending the coroner's inquest peered in to examine the body of Thomas Sinden, butler to Sir John Chandos Reade of Shipton Court.

Shipton Court was built for the Lacey family in about 1603. Sixty years later, it came into the possession of the Reades, whose Berkshire

Shipton Court: built in 1603 for Sir Rowland de Lacey

Sir John Chandos Reade, seventh baronet Reade, high sheriff of the county and champion drinker

home had been destroyed by the Parliamentarians during the Civil War. The Reades remained in occupation for two centuries.

Sir John Reade, seventh baronet, was educated at Harrow and Christ Church, Oxford. In 1814 he married Louisa Murray, a niece of Lord Ellibank. The couple had four children—a son, Compton, and three daughters, one of whom, Emily, was described in the language of the time as an "imbecile".

Sir John's drinking exploits were notorious. After dinner at the old Star Inn at Oxford when he was high sheriff of Oxfordshire Sir John distinguished himself among high sheriffs, so far as we know, by dancing on the table. His wife died in 1821, supposedly of grief. And his son Compton, who got into debt at Oxford owing to a similar weakness to that of his father, died unmarried and childless in 1851. Two of Sir John's daughters also predeceased him, so perhaps it is not surprising that he continued to seek comfort in the bottle.

Thomas Sinden had worked for Sir John for over twelve years by the time that the

The Star Inn

events took place which changed forever the lives of three families. He was probably used to his master's sudden rages. He and Sir John were described as being generally on good terms, but they were known occasionally to disagree.

On Sunday 28th May 1843 Thomas was in good spirits, joshing with the other servants in the kitchen at Shipton Court. At 11.15 pm the dining room bell rang and Thomas made his way upstairs. While he was away, a heavy fall or knock was heard by the servants in the kitchen. When Thomas reappeared moments later, he was bleeding profusely from a wound below the right eye, and "much bruised" about the head.

Mrs Bailey, maid to Sir John's daughter Emily, asked Thomas how his injuries came about. Thomas would answer only that "one blow did it". Thereafter, he refused to expand on this explanation. But his condition worsened, and he complained of great pain from his eye and the back of his head. Had he taken a tumble down the stairs? Why?

Thomas Cheatle, a surgeon, was called from Burford. But, in spite of

Before the incident, butler Thomas Sinden had been in good spirits in the kitchen

Mr Cheatle's expertise in the application of leeches and other remedies, poor Thomas began to fit. He sank into delirium, and at a quarter past eleven on Thursday night Thomas Sinden died, aged thirty-nine. He was buried a week later, but his widow felt that justice had not been served. She had reason to believe that Sir John, who regularly drank to excess, had struck her husband such a blow that it knocked Thomas down the stairs. She informed the coroner James Westell of her suspicions, and a warrant for the disinterment was issued.

At the inquest in the Shaven Crown Inn, the testimony of the only witness to what really happened between Thomas and his master contradicted that of the other servants. The footman, Joseph Wakefield, stated that he was present in the dining room on the evening in question, but saw nothing that might have caused Thomas's injuries. Where the servants testified that Thomas was perfectly sober, and had been so throughout the previous week, Wakefield claimed that Thomas had been much debilitated by drink during the past few days, implying that any fall down the stairs would have been his own fault.

So what had the silent witness—the body in the church—revealed

The fourteenth-century Shaven Crown Inn: known at the time simply as "The Crown"

to the medical examiners? On the right side of Thomas's head were visible marks of violence, including extensive bruising. Under his eye was a wound about an inch in length. In spite of being in the ground for only three weeks, the body was described as being in an advanced state of decomposition. This, it was reasoned, made it impossible to connect the obvious signs of violence to Thomas's head with any cause of death. The jury returned a verdict of "natural death by the visitation of God".

Footman Joseph Wakefield was the only eye-witness to the cause of Thomas Sinden's injuries

The Crown: originally accommodation for pilgrims visiting Bruern Abbey

Convenient though this sounds for Sir John Reade, it did of course put him entirely in the power of the only witness to his actions—his footman Joseph Wakefield. Wakefield's immediate promotion to the post of butler might seem reasonable enough in the absence of Thomas, even though Wakefield would have been considered young for such an elevated position at just twenty-eight. And the rapid construction around Shipton Court of a twenty-foot high wall, as well as the barring of the gates to friends and family alike, might be put down to a reticence brought on by the notoriety that the case had necessarily caused. But why, if Sir John was innocent of any crime, did he re-write his will and leave his entire estate to Joseph Wakefield rather than to his own brother's heirs?

After the verdict, Thomas's body was restored to its grave, and the widow, embittered by her failure to receive justice, had the following accusatory epitaph engraved on her husband's tombstone: "It was a mortal hand that did the deed." It was a direct rejection of the inquest verdict. Mrs Sinden may have been in possession of information from her dead husband, but without the corroboration of the only eye-witness, it was merely hearsay. This left Joseph Wakefield in a very powerful position.

When Sir John died in 1868, he bequeathed Shipton Court, along with every stick of furniture therein, including heirlooms, and valuable family portraits, to his butler Joseph Wakefield on condition that Joseph should assume the name of Reade. Sir John made no mention of his only surviving daughter Emily who was, of course, thus deprived of her rightful inheritance. She had, by this time, been shuffled off to genteel Tunbridge Wells where she lived with a companion and a small staff.

The Reade heirs to the title did try to regain the family estate, but the legal process appears to have been mishandled, with papers filed in an untimely fashion and deadlines missed. The title—but not the estate at Shipton—passed to a branch of the family living in the United States of America. Sir John's nephew John Stanhope Hoskyns Reade had emigrated in the reign of William IV. He then secured his naturalisation by marrying Miss Louisa Walton of Dexter, Michigan, in 1836, and their descendants still live in Michigan today.

As for Joseph Wakefield Reade, sometime footman and butler, he enjoyed the life of the country squire for the rest of his life. He and his family lived mostly in the very agreeable Shipton Lodge set back on

Church of St Mary the Virgin: site of Sinden's exhumation

Shipton Court today: divided into apartments in the 1970s

the west side of the High Street, letting the Court out to various well-to-do tenants. Local newspaper reports regularly recorded the grateful thanks of the Shipton villagers for the kind use of the Shipton Court grounds extended by "Mr Reade" over the years for the benefit of the usual church bazaars, fetes, and croquet matches.

Joseph cultivated prize fruit and vegetables and shared the traditional duties of the lord of the manor with whoever was his tenant at Shipton Court. He served as president of the Shipton-under-Wychwood Conservative Association, and attended meetings of the Stow-on-the-Wold and Chipping Norton Agricultural Society. After his death, Joseph's wife and children took on the mantle, helping with various village jamborees and even appearing in amateur theatricals in aid of the cricket club.

Joseph's son graduated from Oxford university and became a barrister. He sold the Shipton Court estate to W. F. Pepper, a Yorkshire coal millionaire, in 1900. The twenty-foot wall collapsed during the night in February 1889. The fate of Mrs Sinden goes unrecorded.

18
The poisoner of Buscot Park

UNDER COVER OF DARKNESS on a blustery autumn night in 1878 a sad little funeral procession made its way by moonlight up the path to St Mary's church in Buscot. Leading the mourners was a broken man, Robert Tertius Campbell of Buscot Park. Campbell was burying his beautiful daughter Florence, knowing that everyone believed her to be a murderess.

Australian-born Campbell had made his fortune in gold prospecting

Buscot Park: Australian Robert Campbell hoped to become an English gentleman

in his native New South Wales. His dream was to transform himself into an English gentleman, so he packed up his wife and large family and settled eventually at Buscot Park in around 1861.

Buscot Park already boasted a model farm, lovingly created by the builder of the house, Edward Loveden. When Campbell purchased the estate from Loveden's grandson, he determined that he, too, would improve the lives of his tenants by making the estate profitable. His plan to make himself the archetypal benevolent landlord centred on the building of a distillery where the farm's main crop, sugar beet, would be converted into alcohol for export to France to make brandy. He built a narrow-gauge steam railway, a wharf, gasworks, brickworks, and a twenty-acre reservoir fed by water-wheels on the Thames.

But all Campbell's dreams came crashing down when his daughter became the main suspect in the mysterious death of her husband. Florence had been married to up-and-coming lawyer Charles Bravo for only four months when he died of poisoning at the couple's home, The Priory

Campbell's distillery formed part of his plan to provide local employment

Florence Campbell Ricardo Bravo: after one failed marriage and an affair, she longed for respectability

in Balham, south London. And the inquests which followed the death exposed Florence to shame and humiliation.

It was revealed that, since before her marriage to Bravo, Florence had been having an affair with a Dr James Manby Gully, a married man she had met at the springs in Malvern. Family disapproval of her relationship with Gully and a longing for respectability prompted Florence in 1875 to accept the proposal of Charles Bravo. She came clean about Gully and assured her new husband that the relationship was over, but Bravo remained suspicious and jealous. He also resented Florence's decision to remain in control of her own property, as she was now able to do under the recent Married Women's Property Act.

Charles's moods caused Florence to turn to her old friend the bottle. On the night of her husband's death, she and her companion Mrs Cox had between them consumed two entire bottles of sherry at the dinner table—and then, upon retiring to her room, Florence sent her maid to bring wine. Bravo did not let the opportunity pass to make a caustic remark.

Shortly after this Charles began vomiting violently in his room and

Scene of death: The Priory in Balham already belonged to Florence when she married

(Left) Florence's lover, Dr James Gully, and (right) her jealous husband, Charles Bravo

called for help. Mrs Cox rushed to his aid and, in an attempt to remove from his stomach whatever was causing the sharp pain, dosed him with mustard, known to be an emetic. A total of six doctors attended to give their opinions, but to no avail. Three days of great suffering later Charles died, and the post-mortem showed that there were between twenty and thirty grains of antimony in his system.

How could this have happened? Three suspects were in the frame: Dr Gully, of whom Bravo was violently jealous, Mrs Cox, Florence's loyal companion, and of course Florence herself, the mistreated wife. Dr Gully was quickly ruled out on account of an alibi proving that he was elsewhere on the night in question. (In spite of this, his career was ruined by the episode.)

Whispers emerged that Mrs Cox was about to be dismissed by Charles on the grounds of economy. A widow with three dependant children, Mrs Cox could not afford to lose her job. The Burgundy

Housekeeper and companion Jane Cox turned against her mistress in court

Charles had drunk at dinner had been found to be unsullied. But what about the water by Charles's bed? Mrs Cox was the first on the scene and could easily have washed out the carafe and re-filled it.

Once Mrs Cox sensed that suspicion was turning upon her, her loyalty to Florence began to falter. She spilled the beans about Dr Gully and Florence's colourful romantic past. For Florence Campbell had already lost one husband. In 1864, in the same church at Buscot where she was now being buried, she had married Alexander Ricardo of Hockham Hall in Norfolk. Alcohol and affairs ensured that the marriage was not happy, and this was when Florence began her affair with Dr James Gully. Florence and Ricardo separated, but before Ricardo could alter his will he died and his estranged wife inherited his fortune.

In another attempt to deflect suspicion away from herself, Mrs Cox even hinted that Charles Bravo had committed suicide for, she claimed, he had gasped at her when she first rushed to his room: "I have taken poison for Gully. Don't tell Florence." This was a new detail that Mrs Cox had not mentioned before.

Another theory had the victim as the villain. Was Charles slowly poisoning Florence with numerous, small doses of antimony in the form of tartar emetic, in order to get his mitts her fortune? Perhaps before bed he had reached for some laudanum, commonly used to treat headaches, but accidentally swallowed too much. Had he then taken the antimony intended for Florence, mistaking it for an emetic that would induce vomiting and counteract the effects of a laudanum overdose?

Or, of course, there was Florence herself. Her marriage to Charles could hardly be described as a love-match. He wanted her money, and she wanted a nice, normal family. Neither got what they wanted. Charles could not get his hands on Florence's fortune and did not hide his disappointment; instead of having children, Florence had suffered two miscarriages and feared that another would kill her. She began to dread Charles's advances.

A verdict of wilful murder was reached but, as all the evidence was circumstantial, nobody was charged. The public was outraged, suspecting a circling of the wagons amongst the privileged classes. Two years after the murder, by then a social outcast, Florence drank herself to death in Southsea aged thirty-three and was buried by moonlight in an unmarked grave at Buscot church.

The newspapers filled acres of space with illustrated reports on every detail of the Bravo case

Grand Campbell family box-tombs can be seen around the porch...

Her father, poor Robert Tertius Campbell, never recovered from the disgrace. His business affairs went into a decline and he closed his distillery the year after Florence was buried. He died a few years later, his dreams of elevating his family into English high society shattered. He elected to be buried well away from his daughter at Buscot, and now occupies a grave at nearby Eaton Hastings churchyard.

... but Florence lies in an unmarked grave under a tree, now piled with displaced headstones

19
The predator of Nuneham Courtenay

AT EIGHT O'CLOCK in the morning on 24th February 1922, Lord Harcourt's valet Henry Hill entered his master's dressing-room in the family's smart London home in Mayfair. The viscount lay on his back in bed, apparently asleep. The reading lamp was still switched on, with a book placed on the table beside it. Lord Harcourt had neatly stowed his spectacles in their case, and then calmly taken an overdose of a sleeping draught. He was quite dead.

Nuneham House: built for Simon Harcourt, first Earl Harcourt, in 1756

Five years before, in 1917, the Lord of the Manor of Stanton Harcourt, Nuneham Courtenay, North Hinksey, Cogges, Northmoor and Shifford had been made a viscount. Lewis Vernon Harcourt (opposite), a married man with four children, was a pillar of the establishment. As a Liberal MP, he had served in the Cabinet for eleven years, he was First Commissioner of Works, Colonial Secretary, trustee of the British Museum, the Wallace Collection, the London Museum, and the National Portrait Gallery, and a member of the world's oldest-surviving chivalric order, the Knights of Malta.

He was also a rampant chaser of little boys and, if boys were unavailable, of little girls too. Not so knightly after all, then.

Loulou's friend, Reggie Brett

Actually named "Reginald" at birth in 1863 in honour of a university friend of his father's, he was rechristened "Lewis" a couple of months later following the death of the Chancellor of the Exchequer, George Cornewall Lewis. He was known by his friends as "Loulou", and from an early age his behaviour began to cause concern. At Eton the boys were warned to avoid taking solitary walks with either Harcourt or his friend Reggie Brett, Lord Esher.

In time Loulou Harcourt would make an attempt on

Loulou and his wife Mary Ethel Burns

the honour of Reggie Brett's maiden daughter Dorothy—and would then seduce her brother Maurice shortly afterwards. The whole episode is said to have put Dorothy off men for good. "It is so tiresome that Loulou is such an old roué," she wrote famously. "He is as bad with boys as with girls… It isn't that he is in love. It is just ungovernable desire for both sexes."

Somehow, Lewis Harcourt persuaded the fabulously-rich American banking heiress Mary Burns to marry him in 1898. Her parents presented the couple with a magnificent town-house at 69 Brook Street in

Edward James

Mayfair. Loulou Harcourt's proclivities were well-known to the inner-circle but, in a more deferential age, such matters were not exposed by the press. Apparently united, Loulou and Mary presided over a respectable political salon in their splendid drawing-room.

But it was at the Harcourt family's country residence in the autumn of 1921 that Loulou Harcourt made the biggest mistake of his life. Having got away with it for so long, this time he forced his attentions upon the wrong victim. Fourteen-year-old Edward James was visiting Nuneham Courtenay in the company of his mother, the former Evelyn Forbes.

Edward James's mother, socialite Evelyn Forbes: she broke ranks

Forbes had been a mistress of the Prince of Wales, later King Edward VII, and James believed himself to be the illegitimate son of the king.

Loulou tried his luck with the boy, who subsequently grumbled to his mother. In a break with traditional aristocratic discretion, an indignant Evelyn James complained to anybody who would listen, and the matter became dangerously public. Even the police began to show an interest. Such goings-on were all very well if kept behind closed doors, but once they became more widely known, the authorities must be seen to act.

Evidently Loulou realised that the game was up. After an evening of playing patience with his wife and daughter at their London home in Brook Street, Harcourt spent an hour or so in the library checking the draft of a biography of his father by Alfred Gardiner. He parted from his wife at his dressing-room door at around 11.30 pm, and was never seen alive again. In the morning he was found by his valet peacefully dead in his bed, having swallowed an overdose of a sleeping draught known as bromidia.

Loulou never knew his mother; she died the day after his birth

A typically British fudge was concocted whereby it was asserted that Harcourt's heart was historically weak, so a normal dose of bromidia might easily prove fatal in his case without any danger of self-murder being inferred. "Of course, there was not the slightest motive for suicide," averred the coroner airily, "no evidence of any motive whatever." Reggie Brett rushed to liberate Loulou's comprehensive collection of child

69 Brook Street, Mayfair

Nuneham House in the 1980s

pornography, said at the time to be the finest in the world. It has never been seen since.

The house at 69 Brook Street, scene of Loulou's quietly desperate death, was sold to the Savile Club, which has largely preserved and maintained the opulent French-style interiors. Lady Harcourt and the thirteen-year-old heir William left London and retired to Nuneham Courtenay. William sold Nuneham to the University of Oxford in 1948, and the family retreated to their former seat at Stanton Harcourt.

Romantic Stanton Harcourt Manor

20
The Nazi of Swinbrook House

SWINBROOK'S UNITY Mitford—the aristocratic Hitler groupie who put a bullet in her head when England declared war on Germany in 1939. We all think we know the story: poor, deluded Unity who returned from Germany unable to walk or talk, and who for the rest of her life needed constant care. So how come she was seen in the years of her supposed incapacity careering about the lanes of Oxfordshire in her car, conducting an affair with a married RAF pilot? The whole business was very rum.

Unity was the fourth of the six celebrated Mitford sisters born to Lord Redesdale of Asthall Manor and his wife Sydney. Her sisters were

Lord and Lady Redesdale and family: Unity is on the left in the front row

Lord Redesdale moved the family from Asthall Leigh to Swinbrook House, which he designed

prettier and cleverer than she was; Nancy and Jessica were talented writers, Deborah and Diana married wealthy aristocrats, and Pamela—famous as a home-maker, but clearly no slouch intellectually—married one of the twentieth century's most noteworthy physicists. How could Unity possibly stand out as an individual?

She chose to outrage, and her route was Nazism. At her childhood home Swinbrook House, Unity shared a bedroom with her sister, the avowed Communist Jessica. They drew a chalk line down the centre of the room, with Unity displaying posters of Hitler on one side, and Jessica retaliating with posters of Lenin on the other. The girls' elder sister, the beautiful Diana, had scandalised society by leaving her husband for the absurd Oswald Moseley, leader of the British Union of Fascists. Unity would go one better and attach herself to Adolf Hitler.

Unity convinced her parents that she wished to study German, and persuaded them to pay for her to go to a language school in Munich. There she spent her days haunting the *Osteria Bavaria*, Hitler's favourite café. At last she got her wish and an introduction was effected. In an eight hundred-word letter home to her father, Unity described it as the most beautiful day of her life.

Adolf Hitler was highly superstitious. Certain accidental details about Unity persuaded him that she had been sent to him by Destiny. She was born in the town of Swastika, Ontario, while the Redesdales were in Canada prospecting (unsuccessfully) for gold; her middle name was

Unity Valkyrie Mitford

A group of Hitler's cronies at the Osteria Bavaria

"Valkyrie", the name of the Nordic war goddesses; and her grandfather, Algernon Freeman-Mitford, had been a friend of Hitler's idol Richard Wagner, and had translated the works of racial supremacist Houston Stewart Chamberlain, whose views inspired Hitler's *Mein Kampf.*

Unity spent five years in Hitler's inner circle

Unity quickly moved into Hitler's inner circle, attending rallies, visiting his Bavarian retreat the Berghof, and distributing propaganda for the Nazi party. Her rapid progress towards intimacy with Hitler was not lost on his mistress Eva Braun, and Unity's arrival on the scene is one of the reasons sometimes given for Eva's suicide attempt in 1935. Braun wrote cattily of the somewhat heavily-built Unity in her diary: "She is known as the Valkyrie and looks the part, including her legs."

When Britain declared war on Germany on 3rd September 1939, Unity's reaction is part of the Mitford legend. Taking the pearl-handed pistol given to her by Hitler, she went to Munich's English Garden and shot herself in the temple. She survived but, we are told, with the bullet still lodged in her brain.

In December, Lady Redesdale and Unity's sister Deborah went to collect her. According to Deborah: "She could not walk, talked with difficulty and was a changed personality, like one who had had a stroke. Not only was her appearance shocking, she was a stranger, someone we did not know... She was incontinent and childish."

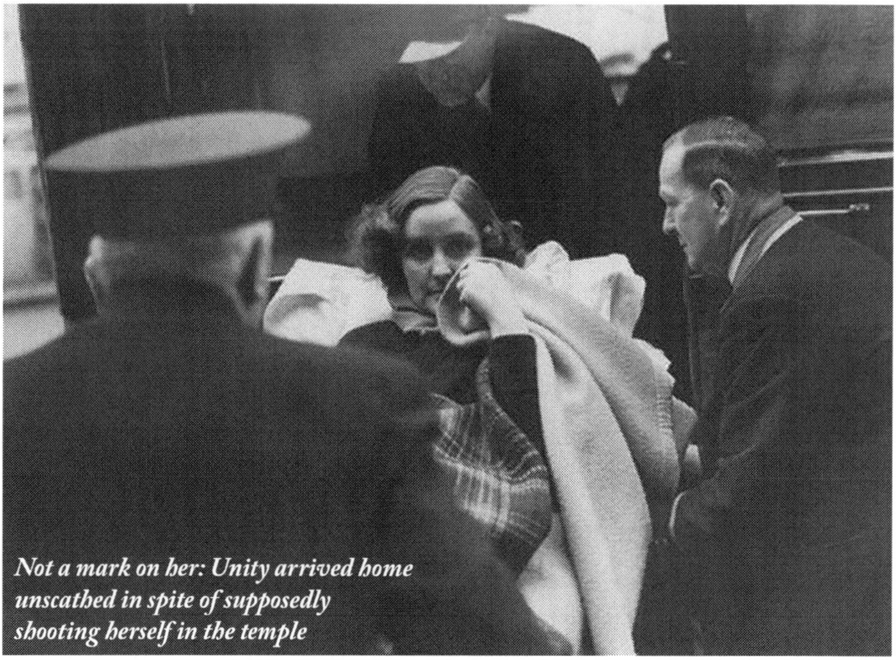

Not a mark on her: Unity arrived home unscathed in spite of supposedly shooting herself in the temple

Could the drama have been staged to evade the normal questioning and detention of known Nazi-sympathisers?

But the newsreel shown at the time of Unity's return to England shows her reclining elegantly on a stretcher, perfectly aware of the cameraman filming her as she emerges from a private ambulance. She has a full head of perfectly coiffed hair with none of the scorching that would normally be seen around a bullet wound, nor any shaven patches such as would be required for proper medical inspection of the site. There is none of the severe bruising around the eyes common to those who survive such a trauma to the temple.

Lord Redesdale's powerful connections ensured that medical examination of Unity when she arrived back in England was forbidden. And, in spite of public calls for her internment as a traitor, nobody was allowed even to interview her as a known Nazi-sympathiser. Some suggested that Unity's dramatic repatriation on a stretcher from inside an ambulance was designed to achieve precisely this "hands-off" reception.

A story emerged in 2007 that Unity had been admitted to Hill View Cottage, a nursing home in Wigginton near Banbury, to have a baby. Not just any baby: Hitler's baby. An investigation of the register of births indeed showed that an unusually high number of births were registered to Hill View Cottage during the war, but none of the entries featured Unity. And a lifelong resident of the village swore to journalist Martin Bright that Unity was staying at Hill View for rest and recuperation following a nervous breakdown, and definitely not to give birth. At the time, having a nervous breakdown would have been just as shameful as having a baby outside wedlock, so the degree of secrecy would have been similar.

Less easy to explain for a brain-damaged woman with the mental capacity of a child is local MP Sir Francis Fremantle's assertion that Unity "drives about the countryside... and picks up airmen." Oxfordshire's Chief Constable Eric St Johnston informed MI5 that, up to 11th September 1941, Unity was having an affair with a test pilot stationed at RAF Brize Norton. He confirmed the identity of the airman as RAF pilot John Sidney Andrews, a former bank clerk and married man with a wife called Irene and a child back at home in Moulsford, Berkshire.

Hill View Cottage in Wigginton

Inch Kenneth: Unity hung the Nazi swastika from the flagpole in the hall

Indeed, Unity was said to boast in the village that Flight Lieutenant Andrews was going to divorce Irene and marry her. MI5 in turn reported the information to Home Secretary Herbert Morrison.

Andrews was hastily posted as far away as possible to the north of Scotland where he died in a Spitfire crash on 1st March 1945. His ashes are interred at Headington crematorium.

Three years later in 1948, Unity died—strangely enough also in Scotland, at the Redesdale holiday home on Inch Kenneth. The diagnosis was meningitis, said to be caused by cerebral swelling around the bullet. She is buried in the churchyard at Swinbrook.

Unity's headstone in Swinbrook

Bibliography

Tim Clarke, *The Countess: The Scandalous Life of Frances Villiers, Countess of Jersey* (Amberley Publishing, Stroud, 2016)

Margaret Dickens, *Chastleton House* (Walker, Stratford-upon-Avon, 1900)

Julie Ann Godson, *The Water Gypsy: How a Thames Fishergirl Became a Viscountess* (FeedARead.com, 2014)

Edward D. Ingraham, ed., *Reports of Cases Argued and Determined in the English Ecclesiastical Courts, Volume 4* (P.H. Nicklin & T. Johnson, Philadelphia, 1832)

Mrs Jameson, *Memoirs of the Beauties of the Court of Charles the Second* (Henry G. Bohn, London, 1861)

John Heneage Jesse, *Memoirs of the Court of England During the Reign of the Stuarts, including the Protectorate, Volume 2* (R. Bentley, London, 1840)

Michael MacDonald, ed., *Witchcraft and Hysteria in Elizabethan London: Edward Jorden and the Mary Glover Case* (Routledge, Abingdon, 1991)

James Moore, *The Tudor Murder Files* (Pen and Sword Books Ltd, Barnsley, 2016)

Thomas Nicholas, *Annals and Antiquities of the Counties and County Families of Wales, Volume 1* (Genealogical Publishing, 2000)

Lawrence Stone, *Broken Lives: Separation and Divorce in England, 1660-1857* (Oxford University Press, Oxford, 1993)

Charlotte Carmichael Stopes, *The Life of Henry, Third Earl of Southampton, Shakespeare's Patron* (Cambridge University Press, Cambridge, 1922)

Charles Sturt, *Report of the Cause Between Charles Sturt, Plaintiff, and the Marquis of Blandford, Defendant, for Criminal Conversation with the Plaintiff's Wife* (J. Ridgway, London 1801)

Edward Topham, *The Life of the Late John Elwes Esquire* (P. Potter, Poughkeepsie, 1815)

C.V. Wedgwood, *The Trial of Charles I* (Collins, London, 1964)

Also by Julie Ann Godson

THE WATER GYPSY

How a Thames fishergirl became a viscountess

AT DUSK on a snowy evening in 1766 a tired young couple made out the welcoming lights burning in the windows of creaky old Shellingford Manor in the Vale of the White Horse, the house that was to be their home. He was Viscount Ashbrook, she was Betty Ridge, daughter of a humble Thames fisherman. Earlier that day they had been married in a little village church, and now Betty—a real-life Cinderella—was embarking on a new life in the alien world of the aristocracy.

NORTHMOOR THROUGH THE YEARS

A FASCINATING collection of photographs, maps, documents and newspaper cuttings charting the history of a village by the river Thames in Oxfordshire and the changing lives of its residents.

MEMORIES OF THE VALE

FIRST PUBLISHED in 1866, this account of rural life in the Vale of the White Horse before the railway came was written by Stanford in the Vale curate Rev Lewin G. Maine. This new edition, edited by Julie Ann Godson, contains many names and occupations useful to family history researchers.

THE SCOURING OF THE WHITE HORSE

FIRST PUBLISHED in 1859, this enchanting novel is author Thomas Hughes' way of recording the very last "Pastime", the festival accompanying the 1857 ceremony of Scouring the Uffington White Horse. As well as giving a full account of the history and sports of the Pastime, this new edition, edited by Julie Ann Godson, also records a lost way of country life when cows were milked by hand, cheeses made on the farm, and the journey to market was by pony and trap. Includes masses of information for family history buffs.

1066: OXFORDSHIRE & THE NORMAN CONQUEST

Why it all started and finished in our county

IT WAS AN EVENT which changed the country forever. And from the birth of a prince to the formal surrender after the Battle of Hastings, Oxfordshire frequently provided the background for the board-room take-over which was the Norman Conquest of England.

www.julieanngodson.com

37060309R00096

Printed in Poland
by Amazon Fulfillment
Poland Sp. z o.o., Wrocław